REALITIES

The Miracles of God Experienced Today

Basilea Schlink

Translated by

Larry Christenson

and

William Castell

Lakeland

LAKELAND

MARSHALL, MORGAN & SCOTT
A member of the Pentos Group
1 Bath Street,
LONDON EC1V 9QA

Scripture quotations, except where otherwise noted, are from the Revised Standard Version, copyright 1946 and 1952 by the Division of Christian Education of the National Council of the Churches of Christ, and are used by permission

ISBN 0 551 00008 2

Printed in Great Britain by
Cox & Wyman Ltd, London, Reading and Fakenham

679041R01

Contents

How did this book come about? I had once mentioned to my 'daughters' in the Mary Sisterhood that I wished our experiences of answered prayer could be put in writing. It would help us remember God's marvelous acts in our midst, so we would ever anew give Him thanks and praise and never forget His goodness toward us. My daughters quietly agreed to fulfill this wish of mine with a special birthday gift—and on my birthday presented me with a book in which they had written down many of our experiences of answered prayer.

One day, some time later, a woman from the United States wrote and asked if by any chance we had gathered together in book form some of our experiences of answered prayer. She knew something about us from other writings, and from having visited us in person. In her letter she wrote, "Through such a book would pulse the theme, 'Praise be to God!' The stories and incidents telling of the wonderful way God works would be an immeasurable help to the timid and uncertain in faith, as well as for earnest Christians who desire to learn the ways of prayer."

Her letter brought to mind the birthday present my daughters had given me. The material they had gathered together served as a starting point for this book, in which we wish to tell you of the wonderful works of God — works we have actually experienced up to this very time.

In preparing this book, above all else I thank the Lord: His Name is "Wonderful"! He has allo 1 us to experience this in real and literal ways. I also want to express thanks to my daughters for the material which they prepared. And my special thanks to Mother M. Martyria, Sister M. Benedikta, and Sister M. Ruth for their help in preparing this book.

Mother M. Basilea Schlink

WE LIVE TODAY in a time like none before. The world is moving rapidly toward a peak of technological development. In all fields man is grasping after the tools of power and control. Yet at the same time we are hurtling toward unimaginable catastrophe. A fear and a horror of that which is coming has, perhaps to some extent unconsciously, laid its grip on mankind. The threat of an atomic war spreads a crippling fear over unnumbered peoples. Mankind stands in the face of the future with no answer. What — or who — will be there to help when catastrophe strikes? Scientists and statesmen have given no answer.

Yet for Christians the dark night of the future is lit by a brilliant star — *the goodness of God the Father*. In the midst of a fear-ridden age, a strangely contrasting word belongs to the Christian: "Rejoice in the Lord always!" Yes, rejoice, here and now at the beginning of the Atomic Age, you who believe in a *living* God who is a *Father* to us in our Lord Jesus. For in our time God, as a true Father, will show us His help and His wonders as never before — if we call out to Him in deepest need, trust Him, and in prayer *actually reckon upon His help*. For He stands ready to help those who believe in His love, who truly reckon upon His almighty power, who truly reckon that He still works miracles today. In the day of catastrophe He can protect us. Through the horrors of an atomic war He can bear us. When we truly reckon with this almighty God, the Father of love, then in the midst of fear we can know the filling of strength and peace.

We have actually experienced the love and power of God, the God who works miracles. We are a small community in Germany, still quite young. Our community came into being through the experience of the war and the judgment upon our nation, especially through the heavy bombing of our city of Darmstadt in 1944. The reality of God in His holiness — but also in His forgiving love — had started a movement of repentance and revival in the girls' Bible classes which we were holding at that time. Over the following three years this led to the founding of our Mary Sisterhood.

From the very beginning, the Lord let us experience His miracles. He did this by time and again leading us, both inwardly and outwardly, to the end of that which was humanly possible. He taught us to wait patiently upon Him, in the certainty that the more difficult the times and the greater the need, the more magnificently He would demonstrate His love and power. We can never tire of praising and glorifying Him for His mighty acts in our midst.

This book, therefore, does not deal theoretically with the idea of a God who works miracles. It is a factual report of that which the living God has actually done. It tells when and how God answered prayer, how He "led us through the deep waters," how He saved and protected us, how He intervened in impossible situations, how He changed human decisions and altered situations and relationships in answer to prayer. It not only tells of answered prayer in common, everyday situations, but also shows God's wonderful intervention in times of crisis and all but overwhelming distress — such as the official decrees from high public offices which seemed to close every door on necessary projects for our service in the kingdom of God. Or again, it tells of miracles in our business affairs, which would baffle any normal system of accounting! A whole complex of buildings on the grounds of the Mary Sisterhood stand today as a testimony to how real was God's help in our business affairs, how literally He answered prayer. These buildings cost great sums of money. We had no savings, nor did we receive any subsidy from official sources. They were built and paid for only through prayer and belief in God's help. And so, through the entire book, this theme resounds: We have a God who works miracles, we have a God who helps! (Psalms 68:20, 72:18).

With a fulness of joy and thanksgiving we share the news: He who trusts God is independent of the shifting tides of politics or economics, or a coming catastrophe. His future depends upon God alone, in whose hands are all things, who speaks a word and brings to naught the hurt or misfortune which would have come upon us by human reckoning. Yes, should even crops and water become poisoned, we can literally reckon upon the words of Jesus: "and if they drink any deadly thing, it shall not hurt them" (Mark 16:18).

Such is the "Song of Songs" which we sing in this book – a life dependent upon the heavenly Father, a life set loose from the many securities of earth, a life bound to God in childlike trust, a life utterly dependent upon prayer.

As I gathered these stories together for the printer, it overwhelmed me anew how safe and certain such a life is — yes, despite all the battles and difficulties of the continuous building projects, the problems of providing daily necessities for many people, and establishing and maintaining various branches of our work with no financial security whatsoever.

These true stories and incidents from our own time confirm that God still stands by the word He spoke thousands of years ago: He who waits upon God will not be put to shame; he who seeks first the kingdom of God and His righteousness will have all other things added unto him; he who gives will receive again in abundance. In short, these stories tell us that he who wagers everything on God, fully trusting in His love and power, will inherit all things. Even here on earth such a faith will inherit all things — a faith which has learned the discipline of obedience, a faith which presents a thing to God and then is able to relinquish it, offering it wholly to God for Him to work out. In times of need you will experience the lack of no good thing. You are a child, utterly dependent upon your Father, utterly trusting Him — and everything is indeed added unto you. For God has compassion upon the small and needy. Like a true Father, He takes their need upon Himself.

And so, the theme of this book is indeed, "Praise be to God!" May it give all who read it the courage to become truly God's *children*, for to such belongs the kingdom of heaven. Children believe what they pray for, because they trust their Father. Children have no other thought in their hearts, but that

He loves them — and therefore of course trains and disciplines them as a true Father — but always sends help and responds to their prayers. And so children truly experience that God is love, pure love, and that He does good to those who wait expectantly upon Him. Children are allowed to experience His miracles. Children here on earth literally experience a foretaste of heaven.

1. God Seeks Those Who Will Pray – A Chapel Out of Nothing!

IN DARMSTADT, on State Highway 3 between Frankfurt and Heidelberg, stands a small chapel. It looks no different than many other chapels. And yet it is different. Why?

At the side of the driveway leading to the chapel billows a large flag on which are written these words: "Built alone through the help of the Lord, who made heaven and earth, through faith in Jesus Christ." This chapel, you see, was built in the name of the Lord—who is called "Wonderful"! It was not built in the usual human way of professional contracting and clearly stipulated financing. It was built, rather, according to the ways of faith and prayer. It happened this way:

In May 1949 the Lord gave me the inner guidance that a chapel should be built—a chapel to His glory in which He would be worshiped and adored. What a strange idea! Shouldn't I first be thinking about some way in which the Mary Sisterhood might obtain a house! At the time, twenty-six sisters were living in the one-family dwelling of my parents—together with my parents and several renters who had been bombed out of their homes. Every square foot of floor space including the attic was being used for straw sacks and mattresses. It was impossible to accept any new Sisters for sheer lack of space. But the Lord had not said, "Because of your cramped quarters and seemingly impossible situation, I will help you build a Mother House." No, the talk was not of our house, but of His House. He burned into my heart the ache in His own Heart, that so few truly worshiped and adored Him.

A little later the thought of building a chapel was posed from another quarter. Mother Martyria and I asked for a Scripture-Word as confirmation. We have a collection of about a thousand Bible passages printed on small cards. After a time of

prayer, we each drew out a card.* These are the verses which
we found written on the cards:

> Take heed now, for the Lord has chosen you to build a house
> for the sanctuary; be strong and do it. (I Chronicles 28:10)

> And let them make me a sanctuary, that I may dwell in their
> midst. (Exodu 25:8)

So God had clearly confirmed our commission to build the
chapel. But the desire to bring true worship and adoration to
the Lord burned but faintly in our Sisterhood. This was pain-
fully apparent at Christmas, 1949. Christmas is surely the time
when hearts should be inflamed and tongues loosed, to join the
shepherds and the wise men in bringing endless adoration to
the Child in the manger. But it was a sad Christmas. The
Baby Jesus waited in vain for adoration.

Afterward a great grief swept over the Sisters. How apa-
thetic they had been in the presence of the Christ Child's love!
And then, out of the ashes of repentance, flamed up the petition, "Let the chapel be built."

With the fire burning in all our hearts, we began to pray
in great earnest about the chapel. Our first object of prayer was
that the Lord would give us the land where the chapel should
be built. We prayed for the most part as a group — prayed
that we would get a piece of land, though we had no prospects
whatever. The more impossible the situation seemed, the harder
we prayed.

Then one forenoon the gong rang out through the house.
Mother Martyria and I had returned from a walk, and our
daughters stood around us. The sun streamed into the room,
glancing off the large iron key which I was gaily swinging in
my hand.

"A key — a key for what?!"

One of the girls burst out, "For a piece of land!"

"Yes, our piece of land!" I went on to tell them, "It's

*In this and similar ways, Scripture repeatedly gave us the clear guidance as to
the path we were to follow — somewhat similar to the practice followed in the
Herrnhut Brotherhood, whose *Losungen* (Daily Scripture Selections) are well
known.

12

on State Highway 3, by a stretch of wooded land. It's close to the city, but has meadows and fields nearby. It covers about one and three-quarter acres — and it's been given to us! The land isn't under cultivation. We can do some planting. And it already has some fruit trees, and even a garden house. Where did it come from? The father of one of our Sisters put it at our disposal."

After weeks of petition, the answer had come. The piece of land was there. It seemed that God had waited until we were aflame with the desire to build Him a chapel, where He would be worshiped and adored. Our lukewarm hearts had to burn with a desire for His Kingdom before our prayer could be "earnest and effectual." We stood there together, overcome — overcome to realize that God had hearkened to our petition and guided the heart of that father to give us the land where we could build the chapel. Overjoyed, we broke into song:

> Now, thank we all our God,
> With heart and hand and voices;
> Who wondrous things hath done,
> In Whom this world rejoices!

Then I prayed to the Father in heaven. If He had given us this land as a promise that we could build upon it — without money, and without subsidy from any forseeable source — would He now give us a word from Scripture as confirmation? That would be solid ground under our feet, a promissory note, which we could take to Him in every need, and which He must redeem. I drew out this verse:

"Our help is in the name of the Lord, who made heaven and earth" (Psalm 124:8).

At this we broke out in a new song of joy and praise. With this Scripture God had truly given us a promise that included everything. It was worth far more than money. Would it be harder for God to bring our chapel and then a Mother House into being, than to create heaven and earth? Surely not! In that moment, the assurance struck deep into our hearts — how easy it must be for such an almighty God, a God who made the heaven and the earth, to bring to completion this building!

13

To us it might seem big, but for Him, how little!

Indeed, this encouragement from His word so strengthened us in that hour that we scarcely gave a thought to the state of our treasury — which at that time contained only 30 Marks!

With this unforeseen gift of a piece of land, we learned that God hears believing prayer, when it is prayed in earnest.

GOD ANSWERS PERSEVERING PRAYER

2. Words of Scripture Fulfilled Today

OUR SISTERHOOD WAS SMALL. We had been in existence barely three years. Most of the Sisters were quite young. We had already encountered opposition from various quarters. We had no influential contacts. We had no money. We had no construction experience. We had no legal advice. We had few friends. Were these the kind of qualifications that would bring the chapel into existence?

We stood before a mountain of questions, uncertainties and impossibilities. Further, the cofounder and spiritual father of our Sisterhood had passed away several weeks earlier. Would the Father in heaven now prove Himself to be a God of the "widows and orphans"? Would He give His children clear guidance? Would He speak to us and if so, how?

One of the first hurdles was the Building Authority. We had to apply for a permit to build on this piece of land. Result: "Under no circumstances can you be issued a permit to build a chapel and living quarters [our Mother House] on this lot. The land is not ready for building. There is no sewage system available to it, and a dug-in drainage system can't be used in that kind of soil. However, there is a partially bombed-out lot within the city limits which is comparable to yours and could be traded. In fact, an old house could probably be included in the trade, with about 38 square feet of living space per Sister."

True it is, "with God nothing is impossible." But should Christians yield right away? Should they let themselves be redirected? Should they renounce what they have begun? Should we persevere with the prayer of faith until the decision of the Building Authority be reversed? Or should we offer to trade this land — this land which we had described in the diary of our Sisterhood as "wonderful, wonderful, wonderful"?

Had not God given us this land directly in answer to our prayers? Was it not like an inner certainty in our hearts, "This is to be the land"?

We called upon the Lord. If this inner certainty were from Him, He could confirm it. His Word could enlighten us in this situation. And He gave this word:

O Naphtali, satisfied with favour, . . .
    possess thou the west and the south. (Deuteronomy 33:23 K.J.)

We went to the window. "Our" land lay directly to the southwest. The land they had offered to trade us lay in exactly the opposite direction. With this word began an earnest week of prayer among all the Sisters. Our heavenly Father already knew that He would need more than one and three-quarter acres for us. Eventually He would need ten times that much — the whole of "Canaan" (see page 101). So here He was not waiting for His children to renounce their plan, and be redirected. Here He waited for their faith, which would battle toward a promised goal.

But all our petitions appeared hopeless. The Building Authority was flooded with building applications, and especially with petitions for new sewers. Every request, every application, every telephone call proved in vain. We could not get in to speak with the Building Director himself. Our petitions got no further than the outside office, where they received the standard reply — we would never get a building permit for this piece of land.

God's hand lay heavy upon us. We couldn't go forward,

15

but neither could we go backward. His promises obligated us to stand firm. God wanted to test our faith, and train us in persevering prayer. But finally the day came when the Lord devised a plan to answer our prayer. It was the end of March, 1950, when the miraculous happened. Mother Martyria tells it:

"I planned to go to the Building Authority yet another time. I prepared myself with much prayer that morning, praying that God would intervene. And then I drew out this Word of Scripture: "(Christ) is the head of all rule and authority." (Colossians 2:10b). I shared this with the Sisters during morning devotions, and added: "It must be that the Lord is going to put a high city official in my pathway today. And then He can prove that Jesus is the Head and Lord of all authorities. Jesus will turn the heart of this official to see our petition as a request for His Kingdom.

"It was a good 45-minute walk from the old Mother House on Steinberg Way to the office of the Building Authority. As I was walking along Steinberg Way, brakes screeched behind me — a motorcycle almost caused an accident. A car came to a stop beside me. The gentleman at the wheel kindly offered me a ride, as it was still quite a distance into the city. It flashed across my mind, *This man is the 'high official' of our city, that the Scripture word spoke about.* And he was, in fact, none other than the mayor! During the five-minute ride I was able to tell him about our request.

"This time, when I came to the office of the Building Authority, my visit didn't end with hopeless waiting in the outer office. The Chief Building Director interrupted a meeting on my account — he had already learned of our situation from the mayor. The mayor had more than fulfilled his promise to 'mention it to the Building Director when the occasion arises.' He had interrupted his many duties and telephoned at once. And what happened? What had been impossible became suddenly possible. The mountains of difficulties melted like wax before God, the Lord of lords. I could scarcely believe my ears. Then and there the Chief Building Director assured us that we would receive permission to build on the plot of land that had been given to us.

"When I returned to the house, I found a letter from the Building Authority in the mailbox. It had been mailed the day before. It was another official *No*.

"But Christ had changed that *No* into a *Yes!* On this day of rejoicing, He indelibly inscribed upon our hearts that He is indeed 'the head of all rule and authority.' In our day also, He has power to change a written *No* of the highest authorities. Such a *No* was meant to test our faith. In the face of it God meant for us not to withdraw in fright, but to hold on in faith. For when His hour came, He acted decisively, and with power."

GOD WANTS FERVENT PRAYER

3. Repentance Clears the Way – Even for a Building Permit

LET US have no wrong conception about miracles. The granting of a petition never follows mechanically, as in a telephone booth when you drop in the second nickel and get a dial tone. To experience miracles means to come in touch with the living and holy God — with the consuming fire which is incompatible with our sins. Since we entered into the realm of this wonderful God through practical discipleship, we discovered that His glorious intervention was almost always preceded by painful judgments and chastisements.

And so it was at this time — before we could actually start with the building of the chapel and Mother House.

"The Lord is near." This call meant an inner adjustment for us during the interim before the building began. We had very little time to get things accomplished, and every day the postponement of the starting of the building was a very heavy load. Was it not necessary in our time, which already bears

17

the signs of "the last days," to achieve in days that which formerly took months and years?

After we received our building permit, we submitted our drawings. Naturally our requests were mired down in the official procedures of the Land Register, Surveying Office, and similar official places, together with the requests of many others. Always something was missing or interfering so that we could not get started. During the continuous trips to the authorities, begging for permission to build, some of us began to get discouraged. Our spirits changed from the original eagerness to something like this: "One just has to wait like everyone else; we cannot push others all the time."

Sister Eulalia, who then had charge of everything connected with the building, remembers this situation especially well. She relates:

"After a serious discussion with our Mothers, I understood that this was not a matter of human restlessness; it was an inner response of obedience to God's urgency. However, if we Sisters would stand against God with our reasoning, saying that waiting was the proper course, then how could He intervene?

"I was driven to deep repentance concerning my resistance. I cried anew to God, confident that His might and help could redeem our hopeless situation. A few hours later — it was July 25, 1950 — I stood again in the office where we had gone so often in vain, but now with a different heart, pleading penitently and steadfastly to God for His intervention. However, I experienced the same headshaking as before. 'It does not go so fast. Half a year is the minimum time to process a building petition. Indeed, it often requires a whole year.'

"Then the door to the inner office opened for just a moment. The Supervisor of the Building Department passed out some papers. The door almost closed again when he added, 'What does the Sister want?'

"The secretary: 'The Sister wants to build at all costs.'

"He: 'Tell the Sister to come in for a moment . . . If you absolutely want to build, I don't want to stand in the way.'

"This was followed by a few telephone calls, and all at once I actually held the permit in my hand. It was absolutely incomprehensible. In the Mother House there followed an outburst of joy and thanksgiving. How our hearts rejoiced! We praised the God who works miracles. He had only waited until we, like Christ, would put to death human judgment which misguides us, and make room for the love which furthers and believes in His cause.

"Later on we heard what was said among the building officials. Such a thing had never happened in Darmstadt as long as the Building Department had existed, that a building permit was issued without the completed plans being inspected – and so fast!"

Naturally we did not have a financing plan to submit, as is normal with all new construction. We could only witness to what had become a certainty in our hearts: the Lord Himself would take care of the financing. In this case it meant that the Father in heaven would provide the missing $61,990 for our $62,000 building. What a spate of unsolved problems we dropped in the lap of those authorities! Unfortunately for this department, the official statutes nowhere provided that the "proven financial source" would be the Father in heaven.

From this time on, however, it must have become an unwritten law. We completed the Mother House and chapel, and dedicated them debt-free. Later we were processing an application to build our "Jesus Workshop." When it came to the question of financing, they said a little wryly, "We assume you have the same financial backer you had the last time?" They approved the application without hesitation. Indeed, the saying went around, "With a backer like that, how can they go wrong? It will be in the safest hands!"

Had we continued to follow the voice of our human judgment, God never would have been glorified in the eyes of the building authorities and contracting firms. Had we stopped pursuing the goal we believed in, had we not stormed heaven with our prayers, then the living God could not have performed His miracles.

This experience etched deeply into our hearts our responsibility to hang on in faith when a situation seems hopeless. For then the name of the Lord can be glorified before many people.

19

4. Twelve Baskets Full!

AUGUST, boiling hot! Our sisters came back from the rubble dump where they had been permitted by the city authorities to gather stones from the bombed-out houses. The sight of them dismayed me. They were not only physically exhausted, but their faces wore a look of sad discouragement. After searching at length, they had found hardly a single whole brick. At the same time I knew that the Sisters at the building site were feverishly waiting for a load of stones, so that they might continue work on the wall. What to do?

I prayed and laid this great need before the Father in heaven. The architect urged us to purchase building stones at once. But we had no money. In spite of much prayer supplication during these days, hardly anything came in. So it became clear to me that God wanted to help us in another way. He wanted to give us the bricks by special ways and means. How He would do this I did not know. But that He would do it, I was certain. For after earnest prayer to the Heavenly Father, asking that He would help His children in this predicament, I received this word of Scripture: " . . . and blessed is she who believed that there would be a fulfilment of what was spoken to her from the Lord" (Luke 1:45). In the Spirit I sensed that He had blessed us by beginning to supply us with bricks, and that now He would continue until the building was finished. A great joy welled up in my heart at this promise from His word, and with it a song which I wrote down at that moment and which then became our daily "building song":

> Faith is a royal power divine
> That makes the song of victory mine;
> Before it, even boulders move,

And open doors I find —
With God nothing is impossible.

The Sisters who had been gathering bricks were also gripped with a new expectancy that God would perform a miracle. They received new strength in prayer, for now they were driven by the faith that can move mountains, according to Jesus' word.

A few days later the feeding of the five thousand came up in our daily Bible reading — the miracle of changing little into much. This inspired a great joy in my heart and a new courage to believe with certainty that we would experience such an increase of building stones. I went out to the building site during the lunch hour. I told the Sisters that I had a great gift, and would unwrap it in front of them. I told them to try to guess what it was. And one of them did, too. It was the word: ". . . and they all ate and were satisfied. And they took up twelve baskets full of the broken pieces left over'' (Matthew 14:20 K.J.). I told them we should apply this in faith to the building stones, and when our chapel was finished there would surely be "baskets full" of stone left over, too. In the present situation, however, this seemed like an impossible thing to the Sisters. Far and wide there seemed to be no building stones to be had. Nevertheless their faith and courage were much strengthened by this word.

No one could imagine now this "rain of stones," this multiplying of bricks could take place. Yet God always stands by His word, that nothing is impossible for the prayer of faith. As I came home in the street car, a gentleman "by chance" sat down across from me. He asked me about the Sisters who were working on the building, and about our entire situation. I told him our story. A few days later a call came. The same gentleman introduced himself as an architect. He said that the day before the city administration had met and it was suggested that some burned-out military barracks be torn down. And suddenly the thought popped into his head: "Give these barracks to the Mary Sisters — they are building and I am sure they can make good use of these stones." The suggestion was accepted. We were given permission to tear down the barracks, and keep the building materials. We found some especially good cinder blocks for the walls of our chapel, and with the left-overs we were able to cover the floors of all our cellars.

In this testing God let us see that He assuredly answers the daring prayer of faith. But further, that He holds back His word of promise until faith is actually ready to "see" its fulfillment. And so we learned that because God is a great God, He manifests Himself in great and majestic ways. Our hearts must see His greatness, and await great things from Him in prayer.

Since then we sing with greater fervency and certainty:

> Faith takes hold of God's sure Word
> And moves His mighty arm;
> Before Him melt the needs and wants
> That could our hearts alarm.
> Money may fail and days look black
> But boldly faith will answer back:
> *With God nothing is impossible!*

GOD WANTS TO BE PETITIONED IN ALL DISTRESSES

5. Prayer Tent – Miracle Tent

THE SISTER in charge of the masonry work on our building site told this story:

"In July, 1950, Mother Martyria came to us on the building site. She told us the Bible story of Nehemiah building Jerusalem's walls. 'All events in the Bible should be expressed in the present tense,' she said, 'because the laws of the Scripture are also valid today.' This led to the thought that we should erect a prayer tent beside the building site, and build the house of

22

the Lord with prayer as well as with the trowel. Since then we have had a prayer tent on our plot of land. It stands forth as a sign of the reality of the power of prayer — of the reality of the Living God who answers petitions and performs miracles today, wherever people believe and pray.

"The Sisters took turns in the prayer tent for quarter hour shifts, in order to hold constantly before God — as the Israelites did — their needs and their faith. They prayed over each thing that was needed for the building work, reminding God constantly who He is: the Almighty One, who speaks a word and it is done, who commands, and it stands fast. Then, as they came out of the tent, they would call to the other Sisters the faith-strengthening word of God.

"The strengthening of our faith was necessary because we were lacking almost everything. Soon after the start of the building, God permitted a great shortage of material to occur. Building materials were requisitioned for military purposes because of the Korean crisis. So now we not only had to petition constantly for money to pay the bills when they came due, we also had to petition God for cement, steel beams, indeed, for everything necessary for the construction of our building.

"One day, for instance, our cement came to an end. It meant that construction would have to be shut down within a few days. No firm could deliver any. In the prayer tent we had prayed for many days that God would send us the cement. At eleven o'clock each day we all gathered together in the prayer tent. On this day we came together with a feeling of great distress, when suddenly an entirely new spirit of faith gripped us. We broke out in a song of thanksgiving, certain now that the Lord would not let this construction be stopped. For He had said again and again that He had a great urgency about this. And, above all, He had put a burning in our hearts that His Name should be made great before the people through this building — that He should be shown as the living God, who works miracles yet today.

"What happened? Just as we were ready to leave — and the construction would really have to stand still from the next day on — a huge truck squeezed through our gate with forty sacks of cement! Even though we had just prayed for this very thing, we found it hard to believe our eyes. We even thought it might be a mistake. But the load of cement was indeed for us. Quite unexpectedly the building supply company had discovered these sacks of cement in an emergency storehouse, and had sent them over to us.

"'Ask and it shall be given to you,' Jesus said. And this we actually experienced at this moment, for God acts according to His Word; He has bound Himself to it.

"Our hearts overflowing with thanks and joy, we sang:

> Prayer can touch the heart of God
> And move His mighty arm;
> The Father will His children help
> And save from all alarm.
>
> The Prayer of faith has power to change
> The darkest day to light;
> And many a want and suffering
> Will vanish from your sight.

"In these economic crises we experienced that God almost from day to day answered the many prayers from the prayer tent, and sent His help. We received all necessary building materials without any price rise, and within a short time, even when good customers were having to wait a month to obtain delivery. Much of the scarce building material was even donated to us. We especially remember the cement blocks, steel rods, steel beams, pipes for gas and water mains. Each time these things arrived exactly at the last moment, so that not a single working day was lost."

How incredible that this little building of ours, the building of this poor little group of young Sisters, who had no normal means for accomplishing it, was not forced to lie idle as was so much construction during that time. What was the secret behind it? The prayer tent. It showed us that prayer accomplishes more than taking advantage of all human possibilities, for even with human possibilities in their favor, many builders were unable to work at this time. Prayer alone accomplishes all things. And prayer must undergird all labor. For all our own efforts at building would not have amounted to anything in this time of economic crisis. Physical labor had to be mixed with prayer. An amount of time equal to a full working day of one Sister had to be sacrificed for prayer. But without time given to prayer, all work is so much lost motion. It is to prayer — connected with a corresponding dedication of action — that the promises of God belong. This is what the Lord showed us during this time of building.

God binds Himself to His word

6. Down Payment in the Same Hour

The walls of our cellar rooms were nearing completion. This was a great joy to us, for here six Sisters had made their first attempt at laying bricks, and had finished the work. But our joy was dampened when the architect told us that the materials for closing in the cellar and giving it a ceiling would cost $1500. Further, it had to be paid in a lump sum. We had no such sum. The ceiling for our cellar rooms hovered before us like an elusive vapor.

I had gone out of town to speak at a conference. The architect called up to tell us that he had an excellent offer for the ceiling material, which we should take advantage of at all costs. It meant, however, that the $1500 would have to be paid within six weeks. Mother Martyria asked if she might think it over for a short time. Her heart felt like it was carrying a hundred pound weight. Where should the $1500 come from in just six weeks' time? The gifts that had been coming in day by day had averaged only two or three dollars; only once had we received more than $10. Now she alone would have to make the

25

decision and assume the responsibility for the payment of this great sum. Prayer was her only refuge. She clung to the word which had been given us for this whole time of building: "Our help is in the name of the Lord."

Then she asked the Lord for a further Scripture, and received this word: "I am watching over my word to perform it" (Jeremiah 1:12b). At once it was clear to Mother Martyria that God had thereby strengthened His firm promise. She consented to the ordering of the ceiling material — though with a trembling heart! Yet, at the same time she was confident that this large sum of money would be there at the right time. The Sisters started special prayer effort for the cellar ceiling.

The next morning Mother Martyria received a postcard from me in which I told that to my great surprise and joy a conference participant had handed me an envelope with $250 in it — a gift from an anonymous gentleman. At that time $250 was worth far more than it is today. After my return I learned that this envelope had been handed to me at exactly the same time that Mother Martyria had prayed in deep distress that God would bring us the money in some wonderful way.

Great joy broke out among us over this experience — joy that we have a God who watches over His word to make it good, who does what He promises. And how much God does promise His children — self-willed sinners though we be. It was almost more than we could take in — to be privileged to live and build under the promises of such a Lord. In the days that followed our hearts and lips sang out,

No one will be put to shame
Who waits on the Lord!

Nor were we put to shame in this matter of the ceiling material. God, who had brought us the first $250, also provided the rest in time for the final payment.

7. The Derailed Dump Cart – Why?

WE EXPERIENCED not only positive miracles but also many negative ones. At long range one sees clearly an open way for a faith project. But then, so it seems to us, God creates hindrances where actually there are none. He closes doors that are wide open for others. He erects barricades. This is something we have experienced again and again, up to the present day.

The reason behind it is that because He loves us, God often wants to give us something greater than the immediate necessity which we pray for. God wants to fill us with His own glory. This is why He created and redeemed us. This is the greatest expression of His fatherly love, for then we can again become the expression of His image. And so He has to discipline us, for we are sinners. Such chastenings become a part of one's everyday experience.

The Sisters who worked on the construction of the chapel told this story:

"We had a heavy dump cart which ran on a small track. One day it started skipping off the track, although we were praying in regular shifts in the prayer tent that God would bless and make successful our construction work. The cart weighed several hundred pounds. It was a troublesome and time-consuming task for the Sisters to get it back on the track each time. This continued to happen, interrupting the work and sapping the energy of the Sisters, until finally the Sister in charge said, 'We can't go on like this. All of you come into the prayer tent.'

"In the prayer tent we prayed together, and asked God to reveal to us why He had taken away His blessing from our work today. And then it came out that . . . here a Sister was harboring something in her heart against another Sister . . . or there one had gotten angry with another. For example, one had worked too slow or too fast to suit another, or one had shoveled sand carelessly and gotten some in the eye of another Sister, or one hadn't cleaned the machinery properly. All this had taken place without being cleansed away. The Sisters had allowed angry judgments and condemnations to creep in and build up tension in our midst. These sins against love stood between us and God and our prayers couldn't go beyond the ceiling.

"Now the painful guilt of these judgments — these sins against love — came to us. We begged forgiveness of one another. We came as poor sinners to God and received afresh His gracious forgiveness. We went back to work — and the dump cart never once jumped the track again!

"Another day the cement mixer stopped. We couldn't get it started again. Everything we tried failed, including the efforts of those who knew something about the machine. It stood idle a day and a half. The Lord had revealed to us that time was precious in the building of this chapel — and every hour counted. So we discerned that He must be grieved with us and therefore couldn't answer our prayers for help. Then He showed us that we had not expressed an attitude of love toward a man who had helped us as a temporary worker. Everyone tried to avoid working with him. We prayed together, confessing this sin, and asking again for the Lord's help. The cement mixer started working again, though nothing outward was done to it.

"We recognized that the basis for God's hearing of prayer is the word of Scripture: 'For the eyes of the Lord are upon the righteous, and his ears are open to their prayer. But the face of the Lord is against those that do evil' (I Peter 3:12)."

These fatherly disciplines along the way shamed and humbled us. When God did not answer our prayers, the entire Sisterhood learned to ask at once, "What dost Thou see in us that hinders our prayers?"

Our prayers in the prayer tent had been fruitless on these days simply because we had not taken seriously what Jesus said about the proper basis for our prayers. So He had to let us learn by experience how seriously He takes his own Word. He will not accept prayers from hearts unwilling to forgive and live in love.

8. Blame for the Rain

IN THE AUTUMN of 1950, in the midst of our building operations, it rained every day — veritable downpours. No one could remember a year like it. Even when it didn't rain in the city nearby, it seemed that all the clouds emptied themselves over our building site.

Our Sisters not only got thoroughly drenched, but the walls couldn't be erected. The bricks slipped back and forth on the mortar, and no progress was made. When it did clear up it was only on Sundays. The working days continued to be plagued by these downpours.

Mother Martyria and I tried to lead our spiritual daughters to the inner conviction that this was an expression from God. But the Sisters who were working on the building site tell it this way:

"We were altogether unwilling to accept this at the time. We didn't want to be blamed for everything. We explained the rain by natural causes which satisfied our reason — even though the Scripture so often states that the weather, the clouds, the waves and the storms are governed by God; that He closes the heavens and opens them; that He gives or withholds the rain for a given area, according to whether He wishes to punish it or not. Of course, our prayers for dry weather could find no answer because of this state of mind.

"One day it was raining hard again, and we fled into the prayer tent and prayed together. Then suddenly one Sister confessed her sin — her resentment toward God — and said that she was to blame for the rain. Others followed. One after another they bowed down in repentance, as God's Spirit pointed out their sins. And, behold, when the last one had confessed the rain stopped. This same thing occurred afterward, on several other occasions. So we experienced something of the truth of this Scripture: And I also withheld the rain from you . . . ; I would send rain upon one city, and send no rain upon another city; one field would be rained upon, and the field on which it did not rain withered (Amos 4:7); if you . . . observe my commandments and do them, then I will give you your rains in their season . . . (Leviticus 26:3,4)."

The Lord had given us something to think about through these rain experiences. Only cleansed hands, only prayers from a meek publican heart, are acceptable to God and will be answered. Would the two masons who instructed the Sisters in the work grasp what had happened? We wondered about that. At any rate a little saying grew up between them. When the first drops of rain would fall, and the Sisters would at once disappear into the tent, they would say wryly to one another: "Relax. As soon as the Sisters get together in the tent, it'll stop."

GOD HEARS CONFIDENT PRAYER

9. That Ridiculous Faith

WE WERE IN NEED of building stones again. The ceiling of the cellar was under construction, and soon we would need cinder blocks for the outside wall of the Mother House. As always, we made our need the object of prayer. The whole Sisterhood pleaded as a single person: "Our Father, Thou who dost not give a stone instead of bread; neither wilt Thou give nothing, now that we need stones!" And God answered.

A woman visited us one day who told us that she had been praying for us ever since she first heard about our building project. And it had come to her that the Mary Sisters would need cinder blocks soon — was that correct? It all dovetailed together. She was traveling to see a friend whose husband had a cinder block firm. She would present the request to him.

We rejoiced. God hears prayer! He had found an instrument for His purposes! And indeed, shortly we received word that this manufacturer wanted to donate part of the blocks as a gift.

Day by day we waited for the cinder blocks to roll in. Many weeks had passed since we had prayed that they would arrive at the time they would be needed. But it seemed that all our prayers were in vain. On the day the cellar ceiling was finished and we desperately needed the cinder blocks, they still had not arrived.

The Sisters who were working at the building site, and experienced this pressing need firsthand, said: "We waited from hour to hour. One of the stone masons who directed our work said, 'This is what happens when you're so impractical. Tomorrow the work will have to stop.' One of the Sisters, bolstering her faith, answered back: 'Our help is in the name of the Lord — this time, too!' At this the workmen only smirked.

"By noon the machinery and equipment was already cleaned up and put away because there was nothing more we could do without the cinder blocks. The two stone masons told us that their 'vacation' tomorrow would be at our expense, since they had been ready and willing to work, but no materials were provided. Our hearts sank in despair. Was God going to let our prayers go unanswered, and allow His name to be disgraced before these unbelieving workmen?

"Suddenly we heard a loud horn. A big truck rolled in — and on the truck, our long-prayed-for cinder blocks! We greeted the truck with songs of praise and thanksgiving. 'All praise to Thee, Almighty God . . .' rang out over the countryside. From the depths of our hearts we sang our thanks to God. Once again He had heard our prayer and shown Himself to be the Lord, the 'Yea and Amen.' We clustered around the truck like we would around a long-awaited and favored guest. The two stone masons stood by, taking it all in. One of them, who had withdrawn his membership from the Church, looked a little sheepishly at the load of cinder blocks — this wonderful work of God. 'You know, a man could learn something about faith here,' he muttered."

Why had the Lord kept us in these straits, waiting for His help until the last minute? Why had He not intervened until after the workmen had already put away the equipment? Their reaction gave us the answer. God had intervened in the hour when everything seemed hopeless. And so the arrival of the cinder blocks was more than an ordinary delivery of building materials. For these workmen it was an overwhelming proof that God had acted.

When God acts in an impossible situation, He becomes greater to us. The more impossible the situation, the more honor that is given to Him. Therefore, in spite of prevailing prayer, He often waits until the last minute before He intervenes. Thus He teaches us to "hold on in faith."

On this particular day the Sisters at the building site, and those of us back at the temporary Mother House, had to hold on in faith one more time. The rejoicing of the Sisters at the building site suddenly clouded over. The driver of the truck reached in his pocket and took out the bill for hauling the cinder blocks: $34.00. The Sisters knew that when they left for the building site that morning, there were only two dollars left in the treasury. But trusting in the God who works miracles, Sister Eulalia sent the driver to the place that then served as our Mother House. We were aghast when he came and handed us the bill. What could we do?

During these minutes, the Sisters at the building site were making supplication to God, trusting that He wouldn't do any "half miracle." And at this very moment the postman arrived with the daily mail, which included some gifts of money. We piled it all together, and counted out $34.00 for the driver, leaving less than a dollar in our treasury. What a Lord! His help was perfect. None of the goodness which He had promised was lacking.

The unbelieving workmen gradually came to faith in God and His mighty works. They realized that the prayers in the prayer tent moved the arm of God. God hears the supplications

of the needy. He comes with His help, and with a marvelous
sense of timing! Yes, God helps us in impossible situations as
no man can help us.

10. "Freely You Have Received – Freely Give"*

WHAT AN ADVENTURE in faith our development was financially!
You can see clearly when you consider the economic position
God placed us in.

In 1949, a year after the currency reform, the first products
of the publishing house and our works of art were ready to be
placed on the market. The question arose, should we actually
sell our products? The cofounder of the Mary Sisterhood, Paul
Riedinger, a Superintendent of the Methodist Church, passed
away at the end of this same year. He had had considerable
business experience, having served Mother Houses of his own
church for several decades. Together with us he sought the
mind of the Lord in this matter, during these last months of
his life. How were the Mary Sisters meant to handle these matters? Should we, like other groups, contract for medical and
disability insurance? Should we set certain fees and prices for
our services, as is commonly practiced?

For the sake of the parents of our Sisters we had to provide
some kind of an answer regarding their daily material care,
and the question of their protection and security. Above all,
however, we had to have an answer for our own hearts. We
mothers bore the full responsibility for our spiritual daughters.
Within me a concept took shape, clear and sharply outlined –

*Matthew 10:8, Berkeley.

33

a mental picture painted by the Sermon on the Mount, that for those who seek first the kingdom of God "all these things shall be yours as well" (Matthew 6:33). A word began to sound clearly in my heart — "Father." He will provide, He will prove Himself a Father to His children, in love and power. But that meant that we, as His children, must provide the opportunity for Him to do so; we must clear the way for Him to bestow His might and mercy. This would bring Him glory. And it was this conviction which God had laid upon my heart like a burning fire, that He will and must be glorified.

How could all this take place? It became more and more clear to me. We must let loose our security and protection; we must surrender ourselves to utter dependence upon our Heavenly Father. This would give Him the opportunity to care for us and show His miracles. It meant the surrender of all security and steady income. We would depend upon Him for everything. By faith and prayer we would stand upon His word, "give, and it will be given to you; good measure, pressed down, shaken together, running over . . . (Luke 6:38)."

Superintendent Riedinger, however, had a somewhat different idea, based on his practice and experience. We had to come together in prayer and seek clarity and a unity of purpose in this decisive question. God's Spirit moved powerfully, and brought us at the end to complete unity of conviction. After we had prayed that He would show us the right way, twice in succession we received this same word of Scripture: "He who finds his life will lose it, and he who loses his life for my sake will find it" (Matthew 10:39). All earthly securities which we might want to cling to, such as earnings or savings, we should lose; thus had God spoken. We took out no medical, disability, or old-age insurance. We set no fee upon our services. Our literary works, our arts and crafts carried no price tag. This meant that now we would be totally dependent upon the Father in heaven. We would walk much more the pathway of faith and prayer, expecting all help from him.

We began from that point to walk in this pathway. It made our Sisterhood truly a fellowship of prayer. Every day we started out with nothing. From a human viewpoint we stood before veritable mountains of worries which had to be prayed away. So we had endless opportunities to present God with the many promises of Scripture — bringing them like an "IOU," asking Him to redeem them. But just as often we had occasion to thank Him for His fatherly help.

We will soon look back on two decades of this way of life, a way of life without steady income and security, a way of prayer and faith, but above all a way of miracles and divine assistance, for which we can never cease to praise Him. How wonderfully the Lord has supported us. Generously, day by day, He has taken care of us, in great things and small things. Along this way of "losing one's life" He has not failed to provide for all the needs of our Sisterhood. When, for instance, in the case of sickness He did not intervene directly and heal through the laying on of hands, then he guided many hearts to donate medicines; doctor's care, hospitalization and operations were given us without charge. So through many years of experience this has become a certainty for us: one can never rely upon God enough; His love and power surpass our fondest prayers and expectations.

Through this experience we have also learned something of what it means "to lose your life," and to live according to the word, "You received without pay, give without pay" (Matthew 10:8). It meant that every day we had to set aside all human ways of reckoning. We had to count on God alone, that He would fill our purse and maintain His work. We experienced this recently when we displayed some of our literature in the front of a little booth we had built for this purpose. We had engaged a printer to print up some small pamphlets of talks which I had given. It had taken all our money to have this done. We set no price on these pamphlets, nor on the handwork which the Sisters had painstakingly produced — Bible texts, pictures and little folders.

Mother Martyria tells what happened:

"A young man came by who was a salesman of religious tracts. He had been told he could take anything he wanted here — it was all free. I will never forget that big black suitcase of his, with yellow leather corners, into which our literature disappeared. The two departed, man and bag, leaving me in dismay. Wouldn't this way of doing things bankrupt us? I clung to our word about 'losing one's life,' in order to keep from saying anything. I pleaded to the Lord to act according to His promise, that He who loses his life will find it. Yes, if we would go this way at His direction, He would not let us perish."

And indeed, God has fulfilled His promise. For where has this way led? As we lead visitors across our "land of Canaan" today, what do they see? They see the Mother House and Chapel; the Jesus' Workshop, the large Jesus Proclamation Chapel, the retreat house for guests, Jesus' Joy; the small Francis convalescent home; twenty-two acres of land, plus all the grounds surrounding our buildings. They also discover that we maintain a house in Israel. And how could all of this have come about? Not through our merits, nor from great contributions or capital or mortgages. No. It came only out of greatest poverty, by means of faith and prayer. God proved that He stands by His word: *Give and it will be given to you . . . Seek ye first the kingdom of God . . . Whatever you ask in prayer, believe that you receive it, and you will.*

During all these years we were able to meet our obligations for the buildings when they came due, so that all of them stand free of debt. And why? Because He Himself moved many hearts to give gifts, to make sacrifices for His work, without us having to make solicitations and collections.

Anyone who sees the miracles of God along this pathway of faith must stand in awe at the sheer reality of His word, and bow down to worship Him. He has proved that He can and will pour out His gifts on His children. But first He must set aside our desire to safeguard ourselves and our people by human calculations. And above all He prevails upon us to expect all things from Him in faith, and to give ourselves unreservedly to His Kingdom.

11. Where Did the Money Actually Come From?

"YOU MEAN that you received no building grants, took out no mortgages, and had no capital?" We were asked this kind of question over and over. A few highlights might help to explain how this took place.

In the spring of 1951 we were in the middle of building our Mother House and Chapel. The bills piled up, and we found ourselves in severe financial straits. The income which we received from gifts and donations ranged between only $15 and $25 a day; our debts were mounting into the thousands of dollars. We had not only risked our name in this undertaking, but we felt very strongly that the honor of God was at stake. Business establishments, local authorities, the press, and the general public knew in whose name these buildings were being erected — and they were interested to see how it would come out. We were told that in the mornings, when the streetcars loaded with sleepy commuters passed by our property, a commotion would go through the car. Drowsing passengers would be nudged awake by the elbow of a neighbor, and all eyes would peer out to see how the building was getting on. For the sake of God's glory it was unthinkable that these mounting debts should stop progress on the building.

It happened that during these weeks I was scheduled to give a lecture in a large city. During this period of distress we had cried out to the Father in heaven, that He would solve this financial crisis. He answered in a miraculous way indeed. Following the lecture a lady said she would like to talk to me. I expected a request for spiritual counseling. The lady, however, related to me a strange experience. The previous week she had felt over and over again that Jesus was telling her, "Give the money in your savings account to the Mary Sisters." But she

37

had said, "I won't do this. In the first place, I don't even know the Mary Sisters. And secondly, I need that money for a rainy day." The day following, however, she developed such severe pains in her legs that she could scarcely walk. She got to wondering whether these pains could be related to the inner "No" she had spoken to God. She prayed that He would take the pains away if that were the cause, for she was now willing to part with her money. And the pains literally disappeared at once. After this experience she came to my lecture.

When she had told her story, she took some money out of her purse and gave it to me for our building. It amounted to $200 — a large sum for us in our present predicament.

This answered prayer in response to our cry for help deeply moved me. God's way of helping in this case gave us a glimpse into His great heart of love, and His ways of working. It showed us His fatherly care for the completion of the chapel. But it showed us something else, too. It showed us that what He provides becomes a blessing to both giver and receiver. Here He had very personally and lovingly pressured one of His children to make a sacrifice for Him which came back to her as a blessing and, on the other hand, was used to advance His Kingdom.

In the months that followed we had to travel dark paths in faith again. According to human reckoning there was no way out. But this little experience became a song of strength to us.

> Thou art a Father, more than a Father,
> To me Thy little child;
> Ways and means Thou always findest,
> My heart Thou hast beguiled!

12. Signs Fulfilled – Sins Repented Of

THE QUESTION of an organ for our Mother House Chapel confronted us. Did we dare order it at this time — or should we wait? It was certainly our hearts' desire, for the chapel should be used for daily worship. So we pleaded fervently with our Heavenly Father, that He would give us an organ for His chapel. It was, humanly speaking, an impossible request. Not only did we not have any money for such an expense, but large debts were still outstanding. So I asked for a sign from the Lord. If, in the coming week, contrary to all expectations, an exceptionally large contribution should be received — say, a lump sum of $250 — then this would be a sign of a "down payment" from God; we would be allowed to order the organ, and He would supply the remaining funds. This took place on a Sunday evening in January. Christmas had just passed, and with it the expectation of special gifts.

The next day a lady from Wurttemberg came to our little guest house, which was a rented apartment in Darmstadt at that time. The Sister in charge of the guest house thought: *Perhaps our guest would enjoy it if I prepared a dish which is a specialty to her part of the country — 'Swabish Spaetzle.'* It's quite an art, however, to prepare Swabish spaetzle. Only natives seem to have the knack for it. So our Sister's effort didn't turn out too well. Our guest picked at the food during lunch, and said, "Is this supposed to be spaetzle?" The Sister took offense at the remark, and gave a sharp retort.

During the rest of the lunch, and especially afterward, the Sister felt very embarrassed about her behavior. In a mood of deep repentance she knocked at the guest's door to ask her forgiveness. The woman also felt very sorry for what had happened, and they were reconciled. Out of this grew up a warm friendship, which has lasted through the years. As she was leaving, this lady took out her purse and pressed $250 into the hand of the astonished Sister!

We were just sitting down to dinner in the Mother House when the Sister entered with her face beaming, waving her stack of bills. The down payment for our organ!

God had answered our prayer. A few months before, when we were in dark days and needed money badly, He had moved a lady through pain in her legs to bring a gift. This time it had been entirely different.

With God there is no set pattern. Many and varied are His ways of answering prayer — even for the same need. We stood in awe at His marvelous and miraculous ways. They are so far beyond our reason. Truly, His name is "Wonderful"! He can use even our sins, when we repent of them, as a means for answering our prayers. Since then we sing with even greater abandon —

> How You will help I do not see
> Hallelujah, Hallelujah!
> But glorious Your help will be
> Hallelujah, Hallelujah!

GOD LOVES CHILDLIKE PRAYER

13. The Daily Devotion for June 20th

OUR FINANCIAL TROUBLES mount — bills for our construction work pile up — but God seems silent — no help arrives!

Our late Sister Angelica had to rest a great deal during this time, because of her illness. At this time of great distress she was leafing through the book of daily devotions and Bible texts put out each year by the Herrnhut Brotherhood. The texts for June 20, 1951 read:

> Who then will offer willingly, consecrating himself today to the Lord (I Chronicles 29:5).

> But she out of her poverty has put in everything she had, her whole living (Mark 12:44).

Suddenly her heart quickened with the thought: "I will pray that someone who reads this devotion on June 20th will make a large contribution for the construction of the chapel." She took this as a daily prayer project. Many other Sisters joined her, and prayed for the same thing. Others, however, doubted whether this particular daily devotion could be taken as a promise for our chapel.

Sister Stephana, who was our treasurer then, tells the story:

"The 20th of June arrived. Of course nothing happened. But I readily explained this to myself—it would take a little time for the money to reach us. I waited eagerly for the mail the next day, June 21st, hoping to see a money order or bank draft. Nothing arrived. Then a few days later something *did* arrive, and I could hardly believe my eyes—a money order for $125, an unusually large gift at that time, and with it the note, 'See Herrnhut Daily Devotions for June 20th. Affectionate greetings!'

"What a joy broke out! We rang the bell and called together the Sisters who worked in the Mother House. The goodness of our Heavenly Father all but overwhelmed us. We sang out gay songs of praise and thanksgiving. For this gift came during a dark time, full of temptations and fears. Our circumstances and conditions had made it seem as though our Father was more against us than for us. And so this 'daily devotion donation' seemed like a greeting which heaven had addressed to us personally.

"Sister Angelica was especially delighted that God had opened His ear to her pleading. And indeed it did appear that He was pleased with her prayer—pleased that she had not only asked for money in a general way, but like a real child had asked the Father in heaven for something specific. Doesn't a human father like it when his child continually comes to him with this or that specific need? Much more, then, should be the joy of the Heavenly Father, for earthly fatherhood is named and patterned after the Heavenly Father. 'When you become childlike in your prayers, then the kingdom of heaven is yours, with all its gifts and treasures.' "

Later we received a letter from the school teacher who had sent us the donation. As she read the daily devotion for June 20th she felt admonished to act according to God's word and donate her entire savings for the construction of our chapel. She hesitated at first and tried to busy herself with her work. But nothing seemed to go right until she went to her desk and filled out the money order for $125. Then she was happy.

GOD LOVES CHILDLIKE PRAYER

14. "Abba, Dear Father!"

FOR A FEW YEARS we took care of a small children's home located on the "Bergstrasse." Sister Jochebed tells about this period:

"By the spring of 1951 our flock of children had increased considerably. Many of them could not afford to pay anything. We had to feed and clothe them by the ways of faith and prayer which God was teaching our Sisterhood. It meant that every day many little mouths had to be fed. And at this time it was not easy. Vegetables were expensive, and our own garden had not yet produced anything. Innumerable cries for help rose up to our Heavenly Father. Many times during the day we would pause in the midst of our work and petition Him for these little ones.

"One day I went into the village to buy some of the things

we needed most. Along the way it occurred to me to visit a lady who lived all by herself, and was quite poor. And what happened? As I was leaving, she asked whether we could use some canned fruits and vegetables. They were just sitting there, she said, and she couldn't eat them all by herself. There was so much that we had to come and fetch it with a small handcart!

"When I opened the shutters the next morning, I saw a sack on the doorstep. It was filled with fresh spinach. A farmer had left it there secretly, as we discovered later on.

"And that wasn't all. In the afternoon a gardener in the neighborhood asked if we would like to come and pick up some leeks; he was going to reseed his garden, and we could have his present supply.

"We adults were overcome with amazement . . . and with thankfulness! And our little children — they had brought their sincere little prayers to God, asking for all the things we needed; now they sat before these heaps of good things, their faces beaming. None of them will ever forget the little thanksgiving celebration we had together. Each child knew that he was the child of the Heavenly Father, specially loved and cared for. They clapped their hands and sang with us: 'My Father, how good Thou art!' It was heartwarming after that to see with what unlimited trust these little ones brought their prayers to the Heavenly Father.

"Another time we ran out of yarn to mend stockings and jackets. We had barely enough money for food, so I always hesitated to buy anything extra. One afternoon, however, I felt I could put it off no longer. After I had been to the bakery, I stopped in at a little shop to buy the yarn. 'One little box doesn't cost much,' I persuaded myself. Quite a few people were in line ahead of me. As I stood waiting, another voice was arguing within me: 'You should have prayed more. Perhaps the Father will still help. You should wait.' Before it was my turn to be waited on, I turned around and went back outside.

"The next Sunday I took care of the children of a very poor family, while the woman went to church. When she came home she went into the next room and brought out a little package. She had recently knit some stockings, and had a bit of black yarn left over which she was sure we could use.

"'Abba, my dear Father,' sounded constantly in my heart. I was ashamed of my own lack of faith. The love of God overwhelmed me. He was indeed a Father, caring for the smallest needs and difficulties of His children. In caring for these children, I found my own relationship of childlike love and trust toward the Heavenly Father was greatly strengthened."

GOD LOVES CHILDLIKE PRAYER

15. Candy on Saturday Evening

WE HELD a children's Vacation Bible School in our house. Young girls came from every part of the country to attend. They had been told in Bible classes about "the God who hears prayer and performs miracles today." They were eager to experience some "little miracles."

During one of the morning prayer times one of them prayed for some candy. It was during a time when candy was quite a rarity; many of the girls had not had any candy for many years. So the other girls joined in the prayer, and asked that the Heavenly Father might provide them with candy in some miraculous way.

The days passed, however, without any candy showing up. It was Saturday evening, and departure was scheduled for Monday morning. No more packages could be expected. The Sister in charge of the Vacation Bible School felt bad. This little prayer for candy had been the first attempt in the life of prayer for some of the children.

At nine o'clock the doorbell rang. The manager of a wholesale store had come personally to make a delivery. He carried a tin bucket and a large paper bag.

"Please do excuse me," he said apologetically. "I'm so sorry, but I completely forgot about your order of marmalade for the guest house. I hope we haven't inconvenienced you. And just to make it right — " He thrust the paper bag forward. It was full of candy.

This little "oversight," which brought a gift of candy exactly on Saturday evening, left the children speechless. Here they had actually experienced that God is a living God, who hears even our littlest prayers. Indeed, God became greater and more wonderful to all of us through this "little miracle" than if He had revealed His power in something spectacular. For this "miracle of the candy" actually showed us the greatest thing about God — the fatherly love and tender concern which He has for His children. It showed us the real greatness of His love. He reigns over heaven and earth. Yet at the same time He numbers the very hairs on our heads. He listens to the smallest petitions of His children, and responds to their tiniest prayers.

GOD GLORIFIES HIMSELF IN OUR GREAT NEED

16. He Is For Us! — An Inspection Celebration

DECEMBER 2, 1950. The beams for the roof of the Mother House were set in place. The foundation for the chapel was ready to be laid. We had many people to thank, so we decided to invite them all to an "inspection celebration" where they would have a chance to see what had been accomplished so far. This included our many good friends, the architect, the city building superintendent and his co-workers, the two masons, the truck drivers, government representatives, and representatives from the various building supply companies

45

We had no room large enough to accommodate so many guests, except the large basement under the new house. This, however, would handle the group quite adequately. We wanted to furnish it with tables and benches improvised from rough lumber. We would cover the tables with white linen, decorate them beautifully, and serve everyone. We would allow ample time in which we could all praise God together.

An inspection celebration is traditionally held when the roof timbers have been set in place, but before the roofing itself has been put on. The house is open to the sky. Our basement room was also unprotected from the weather. Part of it was covered with cement, but part with the kind of bricks that have holes in them, so it was not watertight. We couldn't hold the celebration in the basement room if it would rain.

The night before the celebration a fearful rain storm broke loose. It was so bad that we thought more about the world coming to an end than about our inspection celebration! Early the next morning the downhearted Sisters went to the building site. The rain was still coming down. What could we do? The bricks which covered the basement were soaked from the rain. They would drip for days, even if the rain would stop at once.

The Sisters sought in vain for a solution. Should we cancel the invitations? It was too late for that. They wiped the bricks with rags, but they kept on dripping. Nothing seemed to help.

We seemed utterly defeated. The only thing left for us to do was pray. This was to be our first "celebration" on the building site. We had experienced so many of God's miracles here, and we had expected that He would stand by us now, commanding the clouds. But He seemed to have gone into hiding. We petitioned Him fervently as we set up the tables but our hearts were in despair. The rain dripped on. The guests would soon be arriving.

We covered the tables with linen. We turned the cups over, so the guests would not find them half-filled with rain water. We decorated each table. In the adjacent room we set umbrellas over the cakes. We waited for our guests, still hoping that God would intervene, but having no idea of the kind of help He would give.

At the moment we did not grasp a basic spiritual truth: it is precisely at the moment of complete helplessness, when the need is greatest, that God is close at hand. Surely He who hears the crying of the young ravens for food will also hear the cries of His children. We had felt that God was far away, but actually the Father was near. He let our need rise to the highest possible point, so that we would recognize and actually taste the complete hopelessness of our situation, from every human point of view. For then we would cry out to God as never before. And in turn we would experience that we have a God who works miracles, who answers prayer and sends His help.

And then the miracle took place. As the guests arrived, the rain stopped and did not start again until they had returned home. But the real miracle was that in the basement where the tables were set up not a single drop fell from the ceiling during the whole celebration. In the other cellar rooms it continued to drip in a steady stream from ceiling and walls. A physical miracle for us and our friends!

And it seemed to all of us that God's presence was more powerful in this poor little basement than in any other celebration we had experienced. What a contrast from the terrible rain storm of the previous night! Here in this basement, which still had no floor, we were like a festal congregation. It was as though heaven itself had broken in upon us. Recently one of the honored guests who was with us on that occasion told us that it was one of the most unforgettable hours in his life.

When we look back to that inspection celebration, it brings an awe into our hearts. "How great Thou art, O our God! I know now that Thou canst do anything, and that nothing which Thou hast undertaken is too hard for Thee. Yea, through deep waters dost Thou cleave a path!"

In small things we have experienced time and time again that when God seems to be against us, He is actually working on us, and He plans to do great things with us and for us. When we think back on our inspection celebration, with all the testing and disciplines that led up to it, it is this "for us" that is the miracle of miracles.

17. I Am the Lord Thy Healer – He Who Keeps Thee Does Not Slumber!

WE NEVER LACKED skeptics, scoffers and adversaries for our young work of faith. We felt it a special burden not to give any offense to these eyes that were directed toward us during the entire building time. The skeptics said that our way of building was culpable carelessness and a tempting of God. To use young girls for such work was utter irresponsibility. But, they said, we probably wouldn't come to our senses until some accident occurred. And that would certainly happen before long . . . .

Terrible building accidents might happen on other construction projects and stir no breath of comment. But the honor of God was at stake in our building work, and a single injured hand could be a catastrophe. How many prayers for new strength and protection rose up to heaven — especially from us mothers! We did not participate directly in the building work, although Mother Martyria joined in the actual work twice a week during my long illness in the summer of 1951. Yet the responsibility for this hard physical labor was ultimately ours, and it weighed heavily upon Mother Martyria and me from the beginning. We had started this building in obedience to God, and for His glory. We had ventured out, trusting in Him alone. According to our inner guidance we had not taken out accident insurance, or any other kind of insurance. Would God now permit some accident or mishap . . . . ?

A Sister fell onto a freshly cemented floor in the second story. She broke through, and to make it worse fell right on the edge of a piece of lumber. She was taken to the hospital. The X-ray showed a compound fracture of the pelvis.

This brought us low before God. What was there in our Sisterhood that would cause Him to punish and judge us in this way — even to the extent of placing His own honor in jeopardy? Mother Martyria and I ordered a day of fasting, repentance and prayer. After a night of prayer — fraught with the worst temptations — I struggled through to a clear conviction: this accident had not been given in order to test us through a long time of suffering; rather, it would serve to glorify God through a healing.

It was then a matter of obedience to God's command, and we took the Sister home. We did it, nevertheless, with trembling hearts. It was a great responsibility. The fearful question hung over our heads: what if she should become a cripple for the rest of her life? According to medical advice she should have remained in traction for many weeks. We were taking her home after only two days. I had to sign for her release, accepting full responsibility. The doctor in charge spoke very earnestly to me. "Mental sicknesses may perhaps be healed by prayer, but prayer will never mend a broken bone," he warned me strongly.

At home Mother Martyria and I laid our hands on the Sister and prayed. Some of the other Sisters stood by and praised the victorious name of Jesus.

> Jesus, the power of Thy dear Name
> Shall heal our ills, and lift our pain;
> The power of sickness Thou hast broke,
> Thy broken ones dost Thou make whole!

The Sister stood up from her bed. She had not even been able to move on her bed without excruciating pain, and now she could actually stand on her feet. We looked at her, and for some moments could hardly take our eyes from her. Then we bowed in wonder and adoration before God — a God who indeed works miracles!

Within two weeks the Sister was completely healed, and presented herself to the doctors. This story spread through the country like wildfire. It magnified God's glory far more than if He had protected us from danger and accidents the whole time. Our hearts overflowed with thanksgiving, and with the song,

We had experienced that when God gives a command, He demands a response of obedience from us. This is the "prayer of faith," and so much can hinge upon it. God was able to glorify Himself through this miracle, and magnify His name before the people, only when we acted in obedience to His command, and took the Sister home. This act of obedience cost us dearly, because of the great responsibility involved. We do not experience the miracles of God — which magnify Him and magnify His name — along cheap pathways of faith. They come along pathways of obedience, which can cost one's very "life." So had God spoken to us through this experience.

Why must it be along such difficult ways? Through these we are brought down to the dust — and only then can God's glory be great.

We experienced several other healings during these years, and God protected us under many circumstances. Several times heavy bricks fell on the feet of the Sisters and they were not hurt. One time a stack of cement blocks started to slide. Some blocks weighing twenty-five pounds hit one Sister on the head. She thanked the Father and His angels, and went right on working. It had not affected her in the slightest.

Another Sister was laying cement on the first floor of the building. She lost her balance and fell head first into a well alongside. She landed a fraction of an inch from a strip of lath with rusty nails in it. She came up without a scratch, and no trace of a concussion.

One time a Sister was levelling a freshly cemented floor when she ran across a strangely shaped stone. It was quite firmly embedded, so she had to hammer at it, and finally pry it loose with a crowbar. When she got it out she discovered that it was a live grenade. It had apparently been in the load of sand that was used for the cement. In spite of the hammering and prying, it had not exploded.

Another time a Sister got her hand caught under a dump cart as it fell back into its cradle. It weighed several hundred pounds. The doctor shook his head in amazement: one would have expected all the tendons to be torn, and the hand badly crushed. All she had was a single light flesh wound, which healed quickly. It must have been that the angels put their hands in between.

These are only a few of the highlights from this time. We had offered many prayers — and our friends had prayed with us — asking for instances of His angels' help, so that "you dash not your foot against a stone." He made true His word: "Thou dost beset me behind and before, and layest thy hand upon me" (Psalm 139:5).

One should not look to dangers, but to the living God. In our prayers we should firmly reckon upon His help. We should stand on His promise, that He sends forth His angels in the service of believers (Hebrews 1:14). That is what the Lord made plain to us during this time of building.

God seeks repentance and renewed commitment

18. The Cork in the Bottle

Scripture speaks about the faith that can move mountains. This is far more than merely believing something to be true or possible. It is a divine hurricane. It grips a man. It completely fills him. It lets him think and desire nothing else except that one thing which God has bidden him to obtain. For this, the man gripped by the spirit of faith gives his all. He is ready for any sacrifice. His will is linked to the will of Almighty God. Retreat is out of the question, so long as he is acting according to God's Word. Should God, however, give him to understand that He has changed His plan, he would at once give in.

God was looking for this kind of faith among us, and so He put us on the roadway of faith. But each new stretch of the road which opened up brought a painful awareness of how bound we were by our human ways of thinking and reacting. We would at once begin to use our "common sense," and to reckon with the known facts, or the clear impossibilities inherent in the situation. The laziness and indifference of our human nature does not like to be constantly disturbed by the restlessness of faith.

We had finished the first phase of our construction work. After two and a half years, the chapel and Mother House were completed. About a thousand people had come for the dedication ceremony. In our hearts was a song of praise. Without mortgage, and free of all debts, these buildings stood for all to see. According to human reckoning, the buildings never should have been authorized because of the questionable financing arrangements! Yet here they were, rising up among the new buildings of our bombed-out city, having been paid for more quickly than most others. The bells in the steeple of our chapel rang out over the countryside. Like "those who dream" (Psalm 126), we could testify that in spite of us the Lord had done great things. The local firms were eager to work with us on our next building project. The saying went around in the Darmstadt business community that "the Lord has a good credit rating after all!"

Something had been accomplished. The Mother House Chapel stood there, its bell summoning people to worship services and hours of prayer. The Mother House was completed, with sleeping rooms, a dining hall, and a meeting hall. But the bells were meant for our guests as well as ourselves, and the guests were still being quartered in a rented house three quarters of an hour away from the Mother House. The numbers of our guests were increasing, so that the house was hardly able to accommodate them any longer. Our Mother House had been built to minimum space requirements, and we soon found ourselves crowded for space because of our expanding ministry. The little attic rooms could no longer hold either the paper or the necessary machines for our expanding print shop — not to mention storage rooms for a publishing house. The Sisters who sculptured large crucifixes out of clay had to do their work outside, and every time it rained, their work was ruined.

Since the growth of our responsibilities could not be restricted, the floor space would have to be expanded. It seemed clear to us that God needed more room in order to continue His work among us. Many of the Sisters, however, thought it was quite impossible to consider erecting a building on the ground directly adjacent to our Mother House.

Impossible? Yes, doubly impossible. The national government had planned an important expressway across this piece of land. Its location was strategic for relieving the traffic congestion of our city. On top of this, a large oil company had obtained a binding lease on the land. Its future traffic prospects made it an ideal location for one of their gas stations. We found out that a motel and other service stations were also planned.

The difficulties seemed insurmountable. The majority of our Sisterhood did not even want to start a fight against such odds. After we had investigated the situation, they were ready to give up. After all the battles connected with the building of our Mother House and chapel, we were frankly tired of believing, tired of praying, tired of building. We didn't realize in what great danger we stood — the greatest danger of the Christian life — *to become complacent and lukewarm.* We were ready to rest on our laurels of faith. Peace and quiet for body, soul and spirit, and no more fighting — that is what we wanted. We all but forgot that without fighting there can be no victory. And only where you suffer for something will you experience its joy.

At this time I was traveling away from home a good bit of the time. In a letter I asked how things were going in regard to the adjacent property. The answer came back that the purchase of the land was out of the question because of the reasons mentioned, and that nothing could be done about it at the present time. Then the Spirit of the Lord brought it to me like a flash of lightning — this was naked unbelief, and behind it stood our indifference. We were guilty of betraying the very commission God had given us. I wrote a solemn letter to my daughters.

53

It went right to their hearts, as Mother Martyria reported later on:

"Every one of us sensed at once that this was the Lord who was shaking us and rousing us from our slumber with a good trumpet blast. How could God work a miracle in this impossible situation if we refused to believe and enter into a prayer-battle? It was as though scales fell from our eyes. This had been the 'cork in the bottle' — our indifference and weariness. This alone stood in the way of acquiring the adjacent property. Until this cork was removed, we could never venture even an approach to the City Building Authority.

"This time a 'little conference' was not enough. The Sisterhood prayed far into the night, seeking the Spirit of truth and repentance. They pleaded that the Lord would bring to light anything which stood in the way of God's intervention. And His Spirit did come, causing us to see and confess our sin. We heard the terrible judgment pronounced over us which the Lord pronounced upon the 'unfaithful steward' in the Scripture. Now we would gladly have done anything to build a house for Him, if only He would once more have mercy upon us.

"After this night of prayer and tears from repentant hearts, I ventured the next morning to call on the Building Authority. The Building Director was a very busy man, and normally one would have to wait weeks for an appointment to see him. But when I called that morning, he said he would be able to see us at once.

"At the beginning of our conversation he had all the documents pertaining to this piece of land brought into his office. He explained what the status of the property was, and said that as far as we were concerned the situation was quite hopeless. The national government had already appropriated funds for the building of the expressway. Then, however, quite beyond explanation, he called in his secretary and dictated a letter to the oil company which had a lease on the property. Disregarding previous plans, he told them that the bypass road would now be provided for three hundred feet further to the south. In this way their plans for this piece of property would be

54

eliminated. The Director went on to say that no building permits would be issued for this piece of land, except to the Mary Sisterhood.

"The oil company accepted his decision without argument. With a single stroke the entire obstacle had been removed."

What had happened? It was something so inconceivable that the Building Authority and the City Administration were discussing it for years afterward. When the Building Director himself looked back upon his own action, he was astonished at his audacity. In that hour, however, even without knowing it, he was God's instrument. And later on he was very happy about it.

Our Lord Jesus said: "If you have faith as a grain of mustard seed, you will say to this mountain, 'Move hence to yonder place,' and it will move" (Matthew 17:20). And after this experience we could say: If you do not have faith and have no goal for your faith, because you are complacent and indifferent the "mountains" stay put. Those things which hinder the victory and the building of God's kingdom are removed only by a fighting faith. God wanted a house to be built. When that desire of God met with faith in us, the house was built. We call it the Jesus' Workshop. It houses our print shop, publishing facility, art studio, and quarters for our guests. And from it goes forth the message that "He is able." Yes, He is able to move mountains — or highways — if we are zealous for His Kingdom, and believe. This is the little sermon that the Jesus' Workshop preaches to us as we enter and leave it each day.

19. The Plum Orchard

ON THE LAND ADJOINING the Mother House we planned to build our "Jesus' Workshop." Part of the land belonged to the gasoline station next door. The rest consisted of three small fields. The acquiring of these fields was bound up with many difficulties.

In his epistle James gives us sound advice: "The earnest (heartfelt, continued) prayer of a righteous man makes tremendous power available." (5:16 Amplified New Testament). What do "earnest heartfelt, continued" imply? They mean that you persevere in *expecting* something – you support it, underline it, invest in it. For example, if you are sending an important letter you don't spare the postage. It goes airmail, special delivery, and you probably tuck in stamps for the reply.

In the life of prayer there is also a certain "underlining" and "support" for our prayer – definite outward expressions – which show God how much His answer means to us. When this comes from a humble heart it has nothing to do with forcing one's own will or self-effort, or wagering with God. It merely helps to show the Lord that one's hope is in Him and Him alone. Depending on the circumstances, we will underline our prayers with such things as special offerings, fastings, vigils, and giving up something in some area of our everyday life.

One of the three small fields was an odd-shaped appendage to the property of an elderly woman. It formed a narrow strip of land right through the middle of the plot where our Jesus' Workshop was to be built. For weeks and months we had prayed that God would make her willing to trade her field for another piece of land, or sell it to us.

Sister Eulalia wrote: "I visited the woman many times, and her brother and sister-in-law as well. But it was useless. She

56

maintained that under no circumstances should people give up what they have inherited from their parents.

"On one of my visits the woman was not at home. A little grand-nephew was there and let me in. He led me into his great-aunt's room. I had never been there before. One glance told me that as long as she lived, this woman would never sell or trade her land. The room was crowded with enough furniture for a whole house — most of it dilapidated. In the corner was a bed. The boy led me there, and showed me how the aunt had to use a ladder to get into bed, because she had stacked all the mattresses that she had inherited from her ancestors on top of each other, and slept on the top one. The boy confirmed my suspicions: the aunt had never given up a single thing which she had inherited.

"With that I went home and reported. Our Mothers said that a person so bound to the things of this world could only be freed by 'earnest, heartfelt, continued' prayer. We sensed that here not only our field was involved, but also a soul bound to the things of this world. Jesus said, 'this kind never comes out except by prayer and fasting' (Matthew 17:21). Fasting means not only giving up food for the body. It can also be the surrender of something that has special meaning for the soul and spirit. In some cases this can be more difficult than physical fasting.

"In the next week or two all prayers were underlined with 'fasting.' It gave us the chance to consider where *our* souls might be attached. In our case, we have no 'estate' to manage. With us often it is only a little wooden cross, a pretty picture postcard, a certain personal necessity to which we cling. Or we have anxiety in regard to some spiritual surrender, and think, *Oh, I hope the day never comes when God will ask* this *of me!* In short, we were called to a 'surrender week,' in which each one of us in secret would let loose of that to which she was attached.

"After this surrender week, I once more visited the woman who owned the field — and couldn't believe my ears when I heard her say, 'I'm not too much sad about the land, but it's the plum trees; I do hate to lose the plum trees!' In a word, she wanted to let us have the land, but still wanted to have the plum trees. So we drew up a contract which stipulated that 'everything on the trees' went to her; every year we would send her all the plums produced on this piece of land.''

God had truly done a miracle. He had acted according to His word, and this kind was driven out through prayer and fasting. We were allowed to experience that the prayer of the righteous, as He promises, makes tremendous power available, when it is "earnest, heartfelt, continued." He truly loosed her soul from bondage, so she could give up the field. But besides that, He had purposed a renewal in our hearts. That was more important to Him than quickly answering our prayer. And therefore He first allowed us to run up against so much opposition.

GOD LOVES OUR DEPENDENCE

20. A Print Shop ... By Faith

WE HAVE in the Mary Sisterhood a gay "commandment song." To do it properly, one must dance as he sings. It expresses the blessed joy of living under the commandment "to be as the poor . . . who ever receive gifts." One of the verses goes like this —

> Those who have few gifts to boast,
> Those who need God's help the most,
> They receive from His great store
> Gifts and wisdom evermore!

Sometimes we sing this to visitors as we lead them through our print shop. The various machines produce quite a "concert" also: the Heidelberg Offset Press, the Heidelberg Letter Press, the Rotaprint machine, the trimming, stitching, and folding machines. Our guests are clearly amazed at the accomplishments of the Sisters, and have often said, "they certainly are well trained in their trade." Actually, however, this is not the case. Our whole printing business rests on the secret principle expressed in this commandment song. Sister Beate, the supervisor of the print shop, as well as her twelve co-workers, had no formal training in the printing trade.

At the beginning Sister Beate spent some time in the afternoons visiting a print shop in Darmstadt. This helped her to acquire some basic information about printing, and to learn some of the most important tricks of the trade. Then the school of great dependence and prayer began. All the lack of know-how, training, and experience had to be overcome through faith and prayer. Such dependence makes one humble and small. It drives you to prayer. So we have been quite happy to be the "unlearned" in almost all fields — for instance, the graphic arts, or publishing, or religious drama. This setting aside of technical training, however, is not a "principle" with us, but has been rather a matter of guidance.

In connection with some work I did with the Mohammedan Mission I had prepared some Bible lessons. In the first years of our Sisterhood these were asked for quite frequently. We felt it necessary to take a step of faith and have them printed professionally. This meant that we must have faith that the Father would provide about a thousand dollars. The first printing was soon sold out, but it was apparent that we could not continue to bear the costs of professional printing. Then the thought sparked in my heart, *we should pray for our own print shop and believe for it.* This would expand the possibilities for our mission. And so the fervent prayer went up, that someone's heart would be moved to give us a printing press — right in the midst of our building operations, when our financial needs were most pressing. And the Father answered. One day a small used Rotaprint machine stood before us, a gift from a couple who knew about our work.

We felt that the machine should be put to work at once. The awareness had come to us that we live in the "end times"; the Lord is close at hand. We could not wait for a Sister to come along who was trained in the printing trade, nor put one of our Sisters through several years of technical training. This undoubtedly would have been necessary with some of the machines we acquired later on. But the Lord allowed us to begin with this small machine, so that we could make use of every day — for the time is short.

What could this completely untrained Sister do as she stood before the new machine? There was only one way out, and that was to cry to God. Need teaches us to pray. She experienced this, for instance, the first time she tried to print something in gold. She ran into all sorts of difficulties. In response to her sighing and pleading, the Lord sent an unannounced guest to our house that same day. He was a printer by trade, and had operated a similar machine. He took great delight in working with her late into the evening, showing her the fine points of running the machine.

Yes, God — who is a jealous God — wants us to be dependent on Him. In love He wants to bind us to Himself, and have us do everything together with Him. God showed us again how well things go when we put our trust in Him, seek help from Him, and *expect* it. He not only did not disappoint our Sisters who worked in the print shop. He actually proved Himself to be the best possible instructor. Our printing turned out so well that the salesman who handled this machine took some samples in his case for advertising purposes.

Soon, however, we came to the place where the little machine could not keep up with the steadily growing demand for pamphlets. We stepped out in faith and ordered a Heidelberg letter press. We made an agreement with the salesman to meet each payment on the due date specified. Of course no one knew where the money would come from. (And it was this way with all the other machines we acquired also.) This machine had been the object of many months of prayer. When it arrived we all gathered around it to sing songs of praise and thanksgiving — but also songs of faith. For now we would have to keep on believing that the money for the payments would be there on time. We had to pray, also, that the Sisters could operate these machines, which required far more technical skill than our first little Rotaprint machine. But God had spoken His *Amen* for this way of faith, and up to this day He has let us experience miracle upon miracle.

Every now and then a machine would break down or quit running. Sister Deborah, who usually operates the Heidelberg offset press, reported that one day a fearful bang thundered through the print shop. The big machine came to a standstill.

"We all turned white as chalk. Two metal holders had jumped out of the frame and catapulted into the drive mechanism. The result could have been damage costing several hundred dollars to repair. Generally a print shop carries insurance on all its machines. Then, if anything goes wrong, the insurance pays the bill. We, however, carry no insurance at all. We found that the holder had broken into many pieces. If a splinter had gotten into the gears while the machine was running it could have sprung the whole cylinder. We had narrowly missed this catastrophe.

"For hours we gathered together all the splinters that were lying on different parts of the machine. They had been hurled with such force that the lacquer was chipped in several places on the machine. With trembling hearts, pleading and praying to our Father, we stood together around the cylinder. Finally we ventured to put the machine carefully in gear and test it — to see whether the angels . . . It started to run with its familiar, dull, rhythmic thud. No more crashes followed. It was completely in order. Whenever we tell this story to other printers, they find it hard to believe that we escaped without several hundred dollars' damage."

It was simply the Lord. He hears the prayers of the helpless, those who have no Helper but Him. We rejoiced again in our poverty, and our utter dependence upon the Father. Again and again our distresses drove us to Him in prayer. And then He always let us experience anew His power, His help, His fatherly love. Indeed, had we possessed a great store of training, knowledge, talent, and money, we would have been "poor" nevertheless. For then we would not have experienced the blessing of His fatherly love. It was in experiencing God's provision for us in the many difficulties of our work that we actually came close to His heart. And so indeed —

How blessed the poor, how blessed the poor,
How blessed the poor shall be;
As children from a father kind,
So they receive from Thee!

Everything in our print shop tells this same story. Helpless children receive from the Father everything they need in answer to their petitions; even in the smallest things they experience His miracles. Over one of our presses hangs an old spoiled Rotaprint master, suspended from the ceiling on a string. It has a special meaning. It reminds us that we are in business with the living God. He is our partner in the smallest details of our daily work. He, the great God Almighty, takes a personal interest in our little distresses, the way a human father does with the broken toys of his children. Perhaps this could be a comfort to those who stand in front of a machine day in and day out, as our Sisters do. For it is easy to lose the sense of connection between heaven and a mechanized occupation.

Sister Beate told this story in connection with the spoiled Rotaprint master: "It upset our whole printing schedule. It was before Christmas, 1961, and everything was running at full speed. A large order was due for shipment to the Holy Land. Then the damage occurred, on a Friday. Everyone knows that you can't get a mechanic on Saturday. And on Friday they are usually booked early in the morning. It meant the loss of at least two full working days. We called the service superintendent in Frankfurt, but to no avail: all repairmen had already gone out on their job assignments. There was nothing we could do. I was about to hang up. And then — was I hearing right? — the superintendent's voice came over the wire:

"'Tell me, has this been another one of your prayer projects?'

"His question took me aback. Of course we had been praying — and how! But why should he —

"'Have you been praying?' he asked.

"'Yes we have.'

"'Well, that's something! One of our mechanics, whom we had already dispatched, just came back to pick up some parts. He tells me he will be through sooner than he'd expected, and he can come over to your place.'

"Even this 'worldly business concern' suspected that prayer stood behind this. And so they were able to share with us what a blessing it is to be a child of the Heavenly Father in Jesus Christ. He hears the petitions of His children, and helps them even with a broken-down machine. We hung the Rotaprint master from the ceiling as a sign of thanks."

Repentance brings God's answer

A Sister who works in the print shop tells this story:

"The Heidelberg offset press wasn't running properly, and we couldn't seem to discover the reason. This became, of course, another occasion for God to teach us how to trust in Him. But this time He made another point with us also. I told my co-workers: 'This trouble must mean that something is wrong within us.' It just couldn't be explained in any other way. But they all received this suggestion in silence.

"Shortly afterward it was lunch time. At 1:30 p.m. the machine started to run perfectly. A little later one of the Sisters stopped in front of the machine. She saw that it was running properly now.

"'Since when?' she asked, face abeam.

"We told her, and then it came out. 'Since yesterday there was friction between me and another Sister.' Neither one wanted to give in. But the machine standing idle gave her no rest. After lunch they had a conference with Mother Martyria. Everything was confessed. There was forgiveness and reconciliation. Precisely at this moment the machine began to run again."

God had given our entire Sisterhood a lesson through this experience. His word stands fast: "If you are offering your gift at the altar . . . go; first be reconciled to your brother" (Matthew 5:23-24). If we are living in violation of God's commandments, our prayers cannot be answered. If a machine breaks down in the print shop, this is now one of the first things the Sisters consider. Before they even consider calling a repairman, they pray together, "Is there anything in us — or between us — which grieves the Lord?"

21. Heavenly Mathematics

NEXT TO THE PRINT SHOP are the rooms for our publishing house. One day somebody said to us: "Well, I'm glad you have a publishing house now! Now you'll see what it's like to be in our shoes — figuring taxes, advertising, profit margins . . . . Isn't that so? Don't you have to take these everyday business matters into account?"

Of course it's true that we cannot avoid the difficulties connected with our work, the lack of manpower, tight production schedules, many hours of overtime, the need for accurate bookkeeping, and so on. But the publishing house also stands on the ground of faith and operates according to the ways of faith. We may publish any number of things — new pamphlets, a book, posters, tracts, brochures, song sheets. But the question is never whether we have funds available, or whether the venture will be profitable. Rather, our first consideration is whether we have received a command from God to publish this thing, and whether it will bless the people who read it.

This is a wonderful way of doing business which we have been permitted to adopt, for it always takes God into account. It creates an atmosphere of relaxed confidence. We have only to concern ourselves that the message of God reaches many, that we proclaim His word, that we bend every effort to publish as many books and pamphlets as possible, so that many people may yet be saved and prepared. The Lord Himself will provide the money and the necessary workers, if we but risk the venture of faith.

All literature, except that which is ordered by bookstores, is given without charge. Whether a person gives anything for it, or how much he gives, is a matter of free choice. Some of the literature goes to countries where no currency exchange is possible. Small pamphlets are distributed by the thousands, as tracts. And our printing and publishing work is actually only in its infant stage. An expansion program will require great sums of money to provide more space, machines, and materials.

No wonder that this business operates at a deficit and yields no profits. And yet, strangely enough, we have never missed a payment on our machines or materials. And, in addition, we have seen one building after another go up, and we have acquired the land of "Canaan."

How is this possible? A mathematics professor in our city followed this way of financial impossibilities with great interest. He dubbed it "higher mathematics," by which he meant "heavenly mathematics." Human reckoning bases everything upon profit. But in "heavenly mathematics" the principle is exactly reversed: "Give, and it will be given to you; good measure, pressed down" (Luke 6:38). These laws of "heavenly mathematics" are safer than all human arithmetic, and are eternally valid. This means that he who enters upon the pathway of giving, as Jesus says, will receive all things in abundance.

And so the publishing work can be done in ever increasing measure. The necessary money does not come according to ordinary human planning—for instance, through good promotion or fund-raising letters. It comes by supernatural means. It comes by reckoning upon God, whose power and authority extends also over money. For He says, "The silver is mine, and the gold is mine" (Haggai 2:8).

22. The Bright Blue Bus

SISTER BENEDIKTA reported:

Children crowded around a small, empty goat stall where we were holding children's Bible classes — poor children, varying shades of cleanliness, some quite unwashed. A painful sense of inferiority was written across their faces. From earliest years they had known want and difficulty. Their sad eyes mirrored the struggles they suffered every day, never knowing relief or victory.

In the goat stall we had room for ten children at the most. The others shouted and carried on outside until it was their turn to come in for one hour. We realized that without a larger room we could not carry on our work with such a large gang of children. The area round about had relatively few houses, and we never guessed that so many children were there.

Where could we locate a room? Should we build barracks?

One day I took a piece of blue chalk and drew a picture of an old-fashioned bus on the blackboard I told the children: "Now we are going to pray to the Father in heaven for this bus. And we won't erase the picture until we receive it." It seemed to us at that time that a traveling schoolroom was the only solution to our problem. In this way we could go from place to place, visiting these poor people, and holding classes. Many of the Sisters joined together in praying for a bus.

Among the children there was an immediate division. Most of them scarcely knew what prayer was. Many went along with childlike simplicity, and learned by heart the "prayer for the bright blue bus." Their mothers told us how they prayed to the Father in heaven about it every morning and evening. The other children, most of them a bit older, made fun of it all. They knew better. "God is not going to drop any bus out of heaven," they said confidently.

So this became a real test of faith for us too. Would the Lord hear our prayer, and act in this situation? We did inquire at several German and American motor pools, to see whether perhaps a discarded bus were available, but without success. The drawing on the blackboard was three weeks old, and nothing had happened. But then something did happen — something over which we could only exclaim: "That could be the work of none other but the Father in heaven!"

A man came by one day and asked if it were true that we needed a bus. He had one for sale, and asked if we would like to look at it. That in itself was nothing unusual. There are certainly many old buses for sale. But when we went to look at it, we discovered that it was bright blue, and an out-dated model (a 1937 Open-Blitz) — exactly what I had drawn on the blackboard!

It was relatively cheap — 1200 Marks ($275) with the battery — but this was still a large sum of money for us. But Mother Basilea said: "Even if we could buy it for a song, there is another side to this thing. Having you Sisters always driving this big bus would be a great responsibility, purely aside from the expense involved. So we must pray for a sign. If an unusual amount of gift-money comes in between now and Wednesday, that will be our *Yes* from God that we can buy the bus; if not, then we won't buy it." In that case the Lord would provide another way.

In the next days many of us prayed up a storm. And before Wednesday there came a sudden inflow of gifts, such as we would never normally expect. After Wednesday this inflow just as suddenly stopped. The sign was clear. Because of the child-like abandon of our prayers, God had heard us and given us what we needed.

In high spirits we fetched the bright blue bus. We drove it at once to the first neighborhood area where we held classes, so we could show it to the children. Many were so taken aback that they could hardly believe their eyes. One said, "Sister, will this story get into the Bible now?"

From this time on prayer groups began to form, even among the youngest children. For they had personally experienced who the Father in heaven is — and that He wants to be their Father. From then on every little thing connected with the bus became the object of their prayers — that someone would give money so every rattle could be repaired, that money for gasoline would come in, that no accidents would happen, etc. And God answered these prayers in the specific and literal way that children can understand — just as He had carefully considered their petition, and made certain that the color of their bus would be nothing else except bright blue!

23. Thirty-Eight and a Half Feet

The bright blue bus was here, a gift from heaven itself. We gave it the name "Jesus' Messenger." We parked it between the barracks of the housing project. The children crowded around outside, and came in by groups. Discipline was impossible. The children inside were forever looking out, and those outside were looking in. One thing was certain: our bright blue bus needed curtains!

One of the Sisters who worked in the bus tells how they prayed: "We thought that rust brown curtains would be just the thing. They would make the room warm and nice. The Father in heaven had agreed that the color of the bus should be bright blue. Couldn't He do it again? We prayed for rust brown curtains, and the children prayed with us. Our windows measured thirty-eight and a half feet in length, overall. Of course we had no money to buy that much material.

"Christmas Eve came . . . and there was a package from a big store which had never given anything to us before: rust brown curtain material. It really was genuine rust brown cur-

68

tain material! In great delight I pressed the package to my heart. But some of the other Sisters said, 'This material is too good for the bus. We have prayed a long time for curtain material.'

"But we prayed for rust brown," chorused the Sisters who worked in the bus.

"Finally we struck on the following agreement. We would measure the material, and if it measured thirty-eight and a half feet, then it would belong to the bus, because that was our measurement. If it measured more or less, it would belong to the Sisters who worked at the sewing machines, because they had not measured their windows. With great excitement we found a yardstick and began to measure the bolt of material. At first we Sisters from the bus seemed to be losing. But no, there it was — exactly thirty-eight and a half feet!"

Did the Father in heaven assign the curtains to the bus because He did not want the children to be disappointed? We know that He has special concern for the poor and the little ones. Scripture tells how Jesus once pronounced a "woe" upon any one who would cause these little ones, the children, to stumble. Together with the children we stood in awe before this work of the Lord. The mighty God had concerned Himself about every last inch of the curtain material which was so important for the ministry of the Jesus' Messenger. In answering this prayer the Father made little children out of us grown-ups. He taught us anew to trust Him in the smallest things, and to love Him with tender affection.

24. Surrounded By Angels

SISTER SARAH, who worked on the Jesus' Messenger at a later time, tells this story: "One of the outlying areas where we took our bus was a favorite hangout for teenage toughs and rowdies. A special police squad roamed the area to handle fights, hold-ups, and similar incidents. Nor did these rowdies spare us. In fact, some of the grown men joined right in with them. They tried to frighten us by threatening to light fire to the bus, or by letting the air out of the tires, or by rocking the bus in an attempt to tip it over, and so on. So we never drove out to our lessons in this area without first calling the whole Mother House to prayer.

"One day we had especially asked for intercession prior to leaving. And indeed, not without cause. The troublemakers had planned an attack on us, as we soon found out. A boy who just couldn't be kept quiet during the storytelling time in the bus fetched his other cohorts. A gang of ten men arrived, fellows who were notorious for their fights and riots. However, they stayed a safe distance from the bus, and nothing happened. It was as if they were held back by some power. At evening they turned around and walked off.

"Back at the Mother House we thanked our Sisters profusely for their prayer effort. We had experienced that there is indeed power in prayer. It moves human hearts, and changes situations. We had new courage when next we drove to this outlying area in the Jesus' Messenger. The conviction was strong within us. We are not defenseless against these planned attacks! The power of prayer is stronger than the power of darkness! Their attacks shall come to naught — Jesus is the Victor!

"And indeed, when we arrived, the leader of this gang came up to me and said in a quiet tone of voice: 'Sister, why are you always coming to us? We might attack you one of these days.'

"This man had been in jail several times for attack and robbery. But before any of us could answer him, he added, as though by impulse, 'No one can do anything to you. Is it true that God is with you?'"

GOD WANTS TO BE TAKEN AT HIS WORD

25. Jesus Today – On the Sea of Gennesaret

THE FINANCIAL RECORDS in our office show that for an entire year only a trickle of money came in. We were in dire straits, for many outstanding obligations were falling due. Then, quite suddenly, a change took place, and we were able to meet all our obligations without any further difficulty. This change could only have been the result of "heavenly management." And it was connected with a special experience on the Sea of Gennesaret, in March 1958.

When we think back on that time, we can still feel in our bones the pain of those unpaid bills. We were running behind about $4000 each month. Our Canaan Retreat House, Jesus' Joy, was nearing completion. When we heard during the supper hour how small our money receipts were each day, we felt we could hardly breathe. It was as though a mountain had been laid on top of us, and we were paralyzed. This was a real battle of faith, and the words of our prayer still ring in our ears. Many evenings we came to the Lord and held up before Him the fact that in ten years and ten months He had never disappointed us. He had always arranged for the money to arrive at the right time. Surely in this eleventh month of our eleventh year as a Sisterhood He would not change. He would not suddenly make it impossible for us to pay our bills. He could not now let His name come into disrepute before the people. Day after day, and often into the night, we laid it on the ears of our Father. And we asked Him also to uncover anything in us which hindered Him so that He could not open up the windows of heaven and pour down His blessings of money.

At this time I had to travel to Israel for a series of lectures. I carried the burden of our financial distress in my heart the whole time. On March 23rd I received a letter telling that no solution to our financial difficulties had been found. And yet at that time I knew that the Lord would have mercy upon us. He is our Father and our Redeemer. The darker the pathway of faith, the more wonderful shall be the goal and the harvest. And so it pays to walk the pathway of faith, even when the darkness seems to all but overwhelm us. I wrote in this general vein back to our Mother House.

That evening I spent some time on the Sea of Gennesaret. I rowed the boat out a little way from land. With reasonable certainty I was at the spot where the disciples were fishing when they saw the risen Lord on the shore (John 21). I could do nothing but focus my whole inner being upon what had happened there. The disciples had fished the whole night long, and had caught nothing. They were discouraged — and hungry! Then the Lord appeared to them. And He did not only speak to them comforting words, which they must take in faith. He also intervened miraculously to help them in their immediate need. He not only provided them with a single meal, but He also provided them with a spectacular catch of fish.

And so I asked the Lord that He would put the same question to me that He had put to His disciples: "Little children, have you anything to eat?" For we were now His disciples also, and we were trusting Him to care for us. If our Lord Jesus would not intervene now, we would be in want. And then if someone were to ask us if we had ever been in want, we would not be able to answer, "No, never!"

Could this same Jesus act differently today than He had then? For the glory of His name this was impossible. For how then could we answer the questions that would be put to us?

"Have you ever lacked the necessary money for your ministry, going this way of faith?"

Would we have to answer, "Yes, often; or sometimes, at least, we have lacked the necessary money"?

And so I confronted Jesus on this spot where He had so wonderfully met the need of His disciples. I asked Him whether He is the same today, never disappointing the faith of His own, and standing back of His word, "If you ask anything in my name, I will do it" (John 14:14). In this hour, when our poverty and distress had risen to its highest point, would He meet our need also?

The Sisters at home knew nothing of this hour on the Sea of Gennesaret. But when I returned home shortly afterward they would hardly contain their joy in telling me what had happened. Beginning the next day large sums of money began to flow in, and continued to month's end so that all our bills could be paid. We were not only able to pay for the Canaan Retreat House, Jesus' Joy, but by the end of the next year we were able to start building the large chapel which bears the name, Proclamation. And at the same time we were paying for more than 20 acres of high-priced urban land.

God had indeed heard the prayer on the Sea of Gennesaret. He had not disappointed us, for He cannot.

GOD HEARS THE PRAYER OF THE POOR

26. Little Tests of Faith – By a Cucumber, and Other Things...

To BEGIN WITH we put up our guests in a small rented house in the city. Sister Eulalia was in charge of it. She tells about a young lady who arrived there one Saturday afternoon.

"I sat down with her at the coffee table, and began to tell

her about our wonderful experiences in connection with our building work — how God hears prayer, and makes the impossible possible. Later on she came into the kitchen to help prepare the evening meal.

"'What are you going to cook?' she asked.

"Without waiting for an answer she threw open the pantry door. She saw a single cucumber. It had been set aside for our Sunday dinner. She was the impulsive type. She took it out, and at once began to slice it up.

"I really had to bite my tongue to keep from saying anything. The little fund for our household expenses was empty. Indeed, the funds of our entire Sisterhood were down to nothing because of the daily drain of the building operations. Each day it was like a miracle when we could put food on the table again. I had been especially happy about this big cucumber which I had set aside for the Sunday meal. Cucumbers were something of a specialty for us at that time. Imagine my horror when I saw it being cut up before my eyes. It was to have been something extra special for our Sunday meal. What would I be able to put before my guests now? I thought about what I had just said to this young woman: that God is a Father who cares for us, and works miracles also today. So I decided to take no action to rescue the cucumber.

"My co-workers in the guest house and I prayed that the Father would look in on us and take care of this little difficulty. Had He not made the wine shortage at the wedding in Cana the object of His first miracle?

"On Sunday we were just getting ready to leave for church. Our hearts trembled a little, wondering what we would have to put on the table at dinner time. Just then a boy rode up on his bicycle, waving a basket in his hand. It was filled with fresh beans from his mother's garden. They were delicious."

We had similar experiences in the Mother House. We were once preparing for a great festival, to which we had invited 180 guests. The Sisters who worked in the kitchen had to prepare sandwiches for this large group. But on the evening before the festival, we still had no cheese for the sandwiches. Nor did we have any money to buy it. And this was to be a special "Thanksgiving Festival." We wanted to serve our guests with gifts which we had received from our Father's hand, as a witness of His fatherly goodness. The Sisters who worked in the kitchen enlisted the cooperation of the other Sisters. All day long they were sending "arrow prayers" to heaven, in regard to the missing cheese. It got to be late in the evening, and now the situation was really desperate. And then a guest from Denmark arrived, bringing with him a large Danish cheese, of the finest quality.

One time a Sister came down with a severe illness which left her almost no appetite. The Sister who worked in the kitchen had no money to spend for special foods, but she presented the need to the Heavenly Father. That same evening He sent fresh tomatoes — and it was at a season of the year when there were virtually none to be had. And from another quarter He sent some appetizing little pan fish.

"Your Father knows what you need." "Your Father" — the words rang happily in our hearts. These experiences gave us new courage to continue on our way, confronted each day with the need for food, and relying solely upon prayer and faith. Indeed, after experiences like this, we traveled this pathway of faith possessed by a great joy. For here we experienced the personal love and care of the Father. And when the birds chirped outside, it echoed in our hearts: "You are of more value than they!" Yes, after such experiences, even the birds could preach us a sermon! Truly, God did do much more for us than for them, for we have this great advantage — we are permitted to pray and believe.

And so we continue happily on this way, as His blessed children. Like the birds of heaven, we live from His hand, trusting solely in His fatherly love and care.

27. *Be Not Anxious*

SISTER ANITA is in charge of "household management," which is a responsible position. She must issue the toothpaste, soap, and other small items which each Sister needs, for we have no pocket money. And she in turn is not permitted to buy any of these things.

When she first took over this position she came to me once and said, "We are all out of toothpaste. We will have to buy some."

"Have you prayed for it?" I asked her. "We do not buy such things. If we all pray about this, you will experience something. 'All these things shall be yours as well.'"

A short time later a large box of toothpaste tubes stood in our dining hall, lined up like soldiers in the box, and exactly the number we needed for our Sisterhood. A barber had sent them to us. He had received some pamphlets and wanted to express his thanks. And they came at just the right time, when not a single tube of toothpaste remained in our house.

This is only one of thousands of experiences. For fifteen years now, up to the present time, we have bought no toothpaste, soap, shoe polish, shoes, stockings, linen, towels, handkerchiefs, or similar things. Guests who share our evening meal with us are amazed to see the variety of things stacked up on the middle of the dining room floor. Of course the face of it changes every day. One time a pitch fork will be sticking up in the middle of soap, shoes and bed linen; another time a typewriter will be set down next to the mending yarn and shoe strings. As these gifts are displayed each evening, there will be a little cry of joy from this or that corner, as a Sister sights the very thing she has been praying for. And so she will join in singing, with all her heart, "Father, we thank Thee . . . Father, bless them now!"

And so indeed, all these things "which we have need of" have come to us from His fatherly hand, according to God's own word: "Seek first . . . and all these things shall be yours as well." And they have usually come at the very hour when we have prayed earnestly for a particular thing, because we were in great need. We have experienced that the Father makes good Jesus' word: "How much more will your Father who is in heaven give good things to those who ask him!" (Matthew 7:11). He has given us good things, innumerable good things. For the promise of His Word, that He helps like a father, has not changed. It still stands today.

GOD HEARS THE PRAYER OF THE POOR

28. The Father's Care in Kitchen and Home

THE GREAT GOD ALMIGHTY - is He not too great for us to constantly bother Him about the needs of our kitchen? Is it not tempting God to operate this way — almost as though we were experimenting with the Holy One? This kind of question is often put to us. Surely one may pray for a great miracle where danger and difficulty are clearly at hand — but to bother Him for caraway seed, or salt . . . . ?

We call the various working units of our Sisterhood "little families." Each little family begins the day's work with a short time of prayer together. Each Sister may mention in prayer what she needs for her work, or particular difficulties which need to be overcome. One of the young Sisters in the kitchen prayed day in and day out for spices, for we had none. Sister Adelheid, who supervised the kitchen, thought this was overdoing it a little; it was enough to ask God for the necessary things, without bringing up things like spices, which we could do without. However, she made no point of it. The Heavenly Father, though, did make a point of it. One evening we received a whole carton of spices from someone "who just felt compelled to send them to us." And since that time we have never been without spices.

The little family that ran our laundry stood before a pile of woolen clothing and jackets — but the bucket of detergent was empty. Sister Barbara let the washing lie and prayed incessantly that the Father would give them what they needed. At this time the Canaan Retreat was beginning in the Jesus' Joy House. One of our guests had gone through his factory before he left, wondering if he might bring us something. His eye kept falling on a bucket of detergent, so he finally put it in his car and brought it along. He was not at all certain that God had guided him regarding this gift, or that something else might not be far more necessary for us. The more he thought about it, the more he wondered whether detergent was not a bit too unusual for a gift. When he handed it to us, we were overwhelmed at how God had heard our prayers in this specific situation.

God had shown that when we call Him "Father" it is not just "sound and fury, signifying nothing." This name reveals His inner nature, the nature of a father, who cares and provides. Imagine a business executive sitting at his desk: signatures, directives, dictation, telephone calls, his oversight of the business, his handling of personnel convince us of his intelligence and ability. But now suppose the door flies open and his little boy comes running in, unhappy about something, or hungry. In the midst of all his business activities, the father takes time out for his child. And then we are truly convinced of his greatness, for we see that it is grounded in love. We would have a false image of God if we saw Him only as the creator and governor of the universe. "God is love." He is a father who wants His children to come to Him with even the smallest needs. Indeed, above and beyond everything else, He is love.

29. 5 - 3 = 300

THE LITTLE FAMILY that worked in the office had to see that all records were properly arranged and filed, and for this they needed an endless supply of file folders. But file folders were also an urgent need with other groups. The demand for them never seemed to be satisfied, because we received this item in such small quantities. The office in the Jesus' Joy Retreat House, as well as the Mother House, had presented this to the Heavenly Father for many weeks in their morning prayers.

One day a company delivered five file folders to us. The Sister at the reception desk inquired by phone whether the office had ordered them. One of the Sisters in the office called out happily, "Yes, a long time ago!"

The Sister at the reception desk was a little surprised, because we are not in the habit of purchasing such things. However, this little outburst, "Yes, a long time ago," was only in reference to the order they had placed with the Heavenly Father. And this was in fact the case, as it came to light soon afterward. For no bill came from this company, verifying the fact that some unknown friend stood behind it, with an order from the Father in heaven.

But answers to prayer should not always be kept for oneself. Sister Mechthild, supervisor of the Mother House office, felt convinced that they should share the five folders fairly with the Sisters in the office of the Jesus' Joy Retreat House — indeed, more than fairly, giving them three and keeping only two. At the same time she kept praying for the file folders that they needed, in the firm belief that the Father would supply them.

A few days later two large cartons stood on the gift table in the dining room, addressed to the Mother House office. They contained 300 file folders, in all strengths and sizes. It was

God's answer to Sister Mechthild for the three folders she had given away, for He will be no man's debtor. Some time later we learned that a firm had had this shipment returned by one of its customers. And since it was all packed, and just sitting there, they put a new label on it and addressed it to us, "because they can use almost anything." The 300 file folders came at precisely this time in order that we would understand that a prayer which is undergirded with a sacrifice — even a small one — has the promise from the Heavenly Father that it will be answered.

GOD HEARS THE PRAYER OF THE POOR

30. How The Heavenly Father Furnishes a House

THE LARGE NEW BUILDING on the Land of Canaan, the Jesus' Joy Retreat House, was nearing completion. But there seemed to be no prospect of furniture for it. It was clear to both Mother Martyria and myself that we should adhere to our basic principle. "We will not buy the furnishings," we said. The Heavenly Father had commissioned us to erect this building with its almost sixty rooms, spacious halls, and a small chapel. But it was always up to the Father Himself to put into these houses what He wanted.

We had moved into the Mother House with nothing more than straw sacks, mattresses, cardboard boxes, knapsacks, and furniture for perhaps one or two rooms — though thirty-five or forty rooms were waiting for us, besides the large halls. Then the Heavenly Father had moved upon people. Without their having any way of knowing when we were moving, they began to offer pieces of used furniture, or to send them over at just this time. It was hard for us to comprehend the speed with which the Father had acted, for in a very short time the last of us was able to lay her straw sack or mattress on a real bed.

When this second house was finished it happened the same way. We moved all the pieces of furniture which were suitable for guests from our own rooms, and furnished fifteen guest rooms. For ourselves, we returned to sleeping on the floor. Within fourteen days Heaven had replaced all the missing pieces, without our making any announcement about the time of our move. It sometimes appears to be almost a principle, that one should try to remain materially "poor" with a Father who is so quick to do us good. But the healthy growth, which a continuous building program demands, has taken care of that more or less automatically.

Once these fifteen rooms had been furnished, it was not difficult to figure where the rest of the furnishings would come from. I was in a gay mood when I said to my daughters, "I'm anxious to see whether the Father will let us celebrate the dedication in June without all the rooms being completely furnished. I don't believe He will tolerate that. But we must pray for every single piece."

So while we waited excitedly to see how the Father in heaven would help in this situation, we continued nevertheless much in prayer. Gradually the rooms were filled with furniture. The shipments came from all directions — and again without our making any announcement about the time of our move. The last bed arrived the day before the dedication. Who can describe the joy and thanksgiving which greeted each bed, each little table, each chair? For each one was an answer to prayer. Things which are received in answer to prayer bring a special joy. It is a greeting from the Father in heaven; it lets us know that He is thinking about us, that He has taken note of our needs, and that He hears our prayers. And so it was a joy to us that we were not permitted to go out and buy furniture for the Jesus' Joy Retreat House, but had to expect everything to come by the way of prayer.

For now the whole house has become a witness of His fatherly goodness. Room by room it was furnished with gifts of love, which God Himself had worked in the hearts of those who gave. And it seems to us that no style from any period even closely approaches this "style of God's love" in its warmth and beauty.

31. An Early Inheritance

How should we furnish the kitchen for the Jesus Joy Retreat House? With gas? With electricity? Did we have anything of our own that we could use? We talked the whole matter over one evening. We owned nothing but a small gas stove, which was not adequate to serve such a large guest house. The workmen insisted that we come to a decision, but we saw no way out of our dilemma. In going through the catalogs we came to the conclusion that all kitchen furnishings were way out of our price range. After this conference, we spent the rest of the evening singing songs of faith, storming Heaven with our petitions for kitchen equipment.

A few days later a pastor and his wife inquired as to whether we already had our kitchen furnished. It had been laid on their hearts and they would go to work on it. We were jubilant: "God is pure goodness, He has had mercy on us in our distress, He has heard our prayer!"

The pastor soon came up with something. He found a manufacturer who would actually let us have a complete kitchen furnishing for half price. But for those who have no money, "half price" is actually not much of a solution. So our joy at receiving this message was somewhat dampened. The pastor and his wife would gladly have donated the whole thing to us, but it was beyond their capability also. They considered every possibility, and in the end there seemed to be only one — from a particular individual there was the possibility of receiving an inheritance. If God would now suddenly move this man to release the inheritance while he was still living, then the pastor and his wife could help us. They agreed, therefore, in prayer that the Father should work this miracle. The Father would have to bring the man himself to this rather unusual idea, for of course such an inquiry was out of the question.

And it happened exactly that way. They received the money, and purchased all the equipment for our kitchen. That kitchen has since become a living sermon to us. It reminds us that the Lord has many ways to take care of His children. He is always opening up new and different ways for sending help in answer to our petitions — ways our reason never could have figured out. When the pastor and his wife first came back to us, we were sad because the "half price" which they had secured still left us in a quandary regarding the other half. Who among us would have thought that God would use an inheritance — from a man still living — to provide the necessary money?

It has been said, "love is inventive." The fatherly heart of God is like a deep well that never runs dry. It forever brings up something different, some new thought for advising or helping His children who come to Him in their time of need. In this situation we had experienced it once again.

And so we live with an excitement and a sense of expectation in our hearts, wondering in just what way the Father will meet our need *this* time . . .

32. Provision From the Father's Hand Alone

IF WE WERE GOING to advertise for a cook in our Mother House kitchen, the advertisement would have to run something like this:

> Wanted, one cook. No money available for food or supplies, but generous prayer-support from all the Sisters. Menus usually made out no more than half a day in advance, since we never know what gifts of food we may receive in the next few hours and maintain no regular supply of staples. Must be ready to cook for an eighty-member family, trusting in the heavenly Father who does not give a stone when one asks Him for bread.

You can imagine that such an advertisement would hardly be swamped with applications. Our Sisters who work in the kitchen, however, have gone this way for years, and know something of its hidden joy and blessedness. They can tell you of the many times that a way has been found, or a need has been met, through prayer alone. Indeed, this is the daily experience of all of us. We all have a song of praise to sing to the Father for His goodness.

We came to this way of living at a time of great financial difficulty. It was near the end of the month, and bills amounting to $1,250 would fall due at month's end. God not only provided this amount in a miraculous way, but also provided the money for a very necessary garden machine which we had prayed about for a long time.

Then I was gripped by a desire to become still more dependent on the Father in heaven, to become still poorer, in order to give Him more opportunities to glorify Himself. So many no longer look upon God as a "father," nor expect anything from Him. In our times, perhaps as in none before, there is the tendency toward independence, materialism, and godlessness. I felt impelled to live in total childlike dependence on Him. It was as though God was drawing us to a way of life totally opposite from the spirit of our times. We were to be "like the birds of the heaven," of whom the Scripture says, "and yet our heavenly Father feeds them." Although this had been our way of life all along, now it was to be so in a further way. For now it became clear to me that we should no longer spend money for food. Our daily meals should be prepared from food that would be given to us, plus the harvest from our own garden.

God had dealt with us through the years in many situations. We had experienced how He pours out His blessings when we wait on Him and expect everything from Him. Now we were to experience an even fuller measure of blessing. This meant that we must trust Him in more areas of our life. We must become even more dependent upon Him. And so we started out on this pathway, where "He alone would spread our table" — in order that His glory might be made great.

We have gone this way, now, for more than seven years. We have experienced His blessings day by day. We have actually been fed from the Father's hand, like the birds of the air. And so we want to testify to His goodness. Especially would we bolster the faith of those whose hearts are full of anxiety at the thought of coming distress or times of famine. We have a God "who works for those who wait for him" (Isaiah 64:4). Therefore even the threat of atomic war need not cause us to despair, if we do but one thing: "wait for him."

33. Vacation Sausages . . . And a Luncheon

ONCE A YEAR we have a "Mother House vacation." It is primarily a time for inner strengthening, but also for physical recreation and renewal. Of course the good gifts of God are a part of any proper vacation. No one in the country knows when we hold this annual Mother House vacation. But I prayed that the Father nevertheless would see that during this time the table was well spread for my vacationing children.

There was a pious butcher who lived in the Oden Forest district. Of course he knew nothing about our Mother House vacation. He had manufactured a new kind of sausage, and put it out in his show window. But no one bought it. It must have been that the Lord then reminded him how the people of Israel had always brought the "first fruits" to God as an offering. He picked six large sausages off the hook, drove into the city, and deposited them on our doorstep. From that time on the sausage was a prize item in his store, and sold very well. The butcher learned from this something of the blessing that comes from giving. Those six sausages were not the last "first fruits" which were laid on our doorstep! That this gift should have come on the very first day of our Mother House vacation — is it not awesome and wonderful, the tender care of our Father?

During special festival times a true father will also provide a special festival meal. Since God has permitted us to worship Him as Creator and Father, it is my firm conviction that He desires to show Himself a father in the matter of our "daily bread." For He delights to do good things for His children, to give them special blessings and encouragement along the pathway of the Cross.

So on the evening before my birthday, I announced: "Tomorrow you will have a festival breakfast and a good luncheon. I have asked the Father in heaven to give it to you. And for tomorrow noon I have asked that all of you shall have fruit salad for dessert."

That same evening all the items for the luncheon arrived, including even ham. No one knew where they came from. But what about the fruit salad? By noon of the next day none had arrived. As we sat down to the table, the doorbell rang. It was a delivery of a large portion of fruit salad from a local store. They had received the order from a customer several weeks earlier, and were sorry that they had been unable to prepare such a large order before today. The donor wished to remain anonymous.

In the evenings I had often played the little pump organ, and sung one of my favorite words from the Holy Scripture: "I will rejoice in doing them good" (Jeremiah 32:41). To me — indeed, to all of us — it portrays so vividly the fatherly heart of God. And yet when we literally experienced this in our own bodies, we could scarcely grasp it — such an outpouring of love! God does indeed rejoice to do us good and make His children happy. And so we lifted hearts and voices in our song of thanksgiving: "My Father, how good Thou art!"

In the Mary Sisterhood we had consecrated ourselves to going the way of the Cross. We had taken Jesus' word for our own: ". . . to renounce everything — to lose our life." But many of us had perhaps thought too little that beside the second article of the Apostle's Creed, which tells of Jesus, stands the first article, which tells of God. "I believe in God the *Father* Almighty, *Maker* of heaven and earth." He is the Creator and the Father. And like a father, He takes care of those who leave "house or brothers or sisters or mother or father or children or lands, for my sake . . ," they will "receive a hundred-fold now in this time" (Mark 10:29,30). Because He is a loving father, He gives us a foretaste of the blessings of heaven while we are still on earth — though this comes "with persecutions," along the way of the Cross.

So once again the Father had shown us His bounty, had blessed us and made us happy. And this kindled in our hearts a great joy, and indeed a longing, for the Father's House above. So I began to tell my daughters about the glories of heaven. Just think: for our little festivals here on earth the Father shows such love and concern, and showers us with good things. How much more we will experience in the heavenly festivals and celebrations! Oh, what heavenly blessings — what proofs of the Father's love — await us there! For then He will no longer have to hold back from His desire to do us good. The sins, which He had to punish and deal with here on earth, will no longer stand in the way of His blessings. Truly, we can never write the words too large, we can never return too frequently to them in our prayers: "God is our Father, and He loves us!"

GOD LOVES THE CONFIDENT PRAYER OF FAITH

34. The Canaan Cow

MOTHER MARTYRIA and I were always much concerned about the health and proper nourishment of our Sisters. So for years it had been my wish and prayer that we could get a cow. In February 1960 we were finally able to build a stall. We had planned it for a long time, and we did the work ourselves. It was a large, inviting home for our "Canaan Cow." In faith I already saw the cow moving into the stall, which would soon be completed. I believe this is a basic spiritual principle. When God gives a promise, and you "see" it in faith, then He will bring it literally into sight in His time. However, as the stall neared completion, there seemed no prospect whatever of receiving a cow. Only our goats seemed to enjoy the move from their makeshift quarters.

At this time Sister Divina had an assignment in a country parish, participating in a week-long Bible school. During the week she also told about our work in the Mary Sisterhood. She showed slides and told about the wonderful ways God had led us. At the end of the program, when everyone had left the parish hall, a man came up and asked the pastor: "Tell me, Pastor, is it true that the Sisters need a cow?"

"Why, yes, indeed, that is true," the pastor replied.

"Then they can have ours!"

It seemed unbelievable, and yet it was so. He wanted to give us his only cow, which was soon to calve. The whole family had been contemplating this all week long. Even the grandmother, who dearly loved the beautiful black and white cow, was willing to part with it.

"Ja, give her to the Sisters, for the Lord's sake," she had said

Sister Divina, and later all of us, could hardly believe it. And we really did not want to accept it, for it was the man's only cow, and precious to him. But he insisted that "God wanted it that way."

So our "Canaan Cow" moved into her beautiful, newly built stall. All the Sisters greeted her with songs of joy and thanksgiving. A short time later a whole group of people from that parish crowded in and around the stall. They had come on a bus for one of our "Proclamation Plays," and they wanted to share our joy and thanksgiving.

It overwhelmed us that God had answered this prayer also and had given us the cow. We can only testify that we can scarcely recall a request which He had not answered. The innumerable requests for daily bread which we have sent up to Heaven — yes, including even the cow — the Father has answered them all. How blessed we are, to be allowed to pray!

35. He Gives the Young Ravens Their Food

OUR "CANAAN COW" thrived, but she had a tremendous appetite! Our lawns were soon eaten up. And then suddenly we were in real trouble, because a great heat wave set in. Everything dried up, and the little grass which was left turned brown. We had no money to buy feed. Our Sisters who worked in the garden scoured the edges of the forest and the roadsides for little patches of grass for our cow. Their hearts cried out: "Father, Thou hast given us the cow! Surely Thou canst not let her die of hunger!" All of us besought the Father in heaven, that He who hears the crying of the young ravens for food, would also take care of our cow. But He kept us waiting. And we thanked Him for every day that we were able to gather together enough food so that our cow survived.

One day our Sister Agathe went out to mow some of the dried up grass on the meadows of Canaan. She wondered whether the cow would be able to eat it. A farmer drove by in his wagon, and he likely wondered about it too. A little further on — he told us about it later — a woman stopped him and asked whether he knew anyone who would cut the grass in her large fruit orchard. It might be that someone would be happy to do it for the feed. The farmer told her what he had just seen driving by our place, and the next day he came and told us about the offer. Sister Agathe could hardly contain her joy. From all of us there went up a chorus of thanksgiving, to a Father who so cares for His children. We were not only able to get grass for our immediate need, but for the whole winter. And it was all free. This experience greatly encouraged our faith in regard to all the needs of our garden and animals.

However, we still needed one thing for the winter: fodder beets. The cow couldn't get along only on hay. We were told that we should figure on about five tons of fodder beets for the winter. The Sisters who worked in the garden brought this request to the Heavenly Father every morning. And the request became more urgent when they discovered that the small planting of fodder beets which they had put in after the cow came had been eaten by rabbits.

Then we received a letter from the parents of one of our Sisters. It said we could come and pick up a ton of fodder beets from their farm. A week later two farmers from a neighboring village delivered two wagon loads of fodder beets — approximately three tons. They knew that we had received a cow, and they said, "We want to give our tithe, too."

In the newspapers these days we read much about the stockpiling of atomic weapons, about test explosions, and their devastating effects on nature. A war that would cost millions of lives is a terrible prospect in itself. But the experts say that more frightful still will be the starvation of those who climb out of their bomb shelters into a desert where nothing will grow because of the deadly atomic dust. This can put a real fear in our hearts.

But against this fear, our day to day experiences with the living God and His miracles have become a great consolation. Times of disaster well may come, that we know. But this we also know: It is the nature of God to perform miracles. He can let water spring up out of the desert at His command. He can feed us with manna if we believe in Him and ask Him. When human reason has exhausted every possibility, the children can go to their Father and receive all they need.

And so we are thankful that He has led us this way of faith and prayer, allowing us to experience His miracles. They are a preparation for the times of distress which lie before us. For only when you have become utterly dependent upon prayer and faith, only when all human possibilities have been exhausted, can you begin to reckon that God will intervene and work His miracles.

36. Not By Our Ways

GUESTS WHO VISIT us and are given a tour of our grounds, will sometimes take one of the Sisters aside and say: "Now just between us, Sister, tell me quite frankly — is it actually true that the money was always there at just the right minute . . or did it happen differently sometimes?"

The Sister will answer, "Oh, yes, always! One time, however . . . but that is something you should hear from Sister Anita herself . . . "

"This happened when three farmers, all at the same time, had promised to sell us their fields. We were delighted, and yet a bit uneasy. Especially when the city authorities immediately approved the purchase agreements, and returned them to us. This usually requires a longer wait. For us it meant that the first installment to all three had to be paid at once. It amounted to about a thousand dollars in all. We had no money in our bank account. Our cash on hand was enough for a full payment to one farmer, half a payment to the second, and none to the third. Of course we came together in the Assembly Hall for prayer. We pleaded with God to reveal any obstacles which prevented Him from 'opening the windows of heaven' and giving us the money. But no answer came, and a great sadness spread over us. For ten years we had been able to say that the Lord always intervened — even if it was at the last moment. It was Saturday. For the first time I was going out to take care of a money matter not knowing what I would be able to say. For during our long negotiations about the sale of the fields, we had emphasized that the farmers would receive their money on the hour that it was due — that God had always been faithful with us in these matters.

"For the first farmer I had the full payment. He could not

92

know how heavy my heart was as I counted out the full amount on his table. But the second farmer — ? I rang the bell, but no one answered. The neighbor lady said he wasn't home. I left a note behind saying that I had been there, and asked whether he could come to the Mother House on his return to get his money. Despite the relief of this unexpected 'grace period,' my heart was uneasy as I approached the third farmer's house. I had no idea how he would react when I offered him only half a payment. But wonder of wonders — I could hardly believe it — he, too, had gone away this particular afternoon. His wife said that he would come to the Mother House on Monday. Quite overwhelmed at God's way of helping and leading, I headed for home. By Monday the amount due the third farmer had come in. When the second farmer returned from his trip a few days later we were able to pay him also."

Why did God do it in such an unusual way, so that the money was there on time even after the "last hour" had passed? He wanted to show us that He has many different ways of helping us. We should not lose courage if the help does not come in the particular way we had expected. But, above all, God wanted to test our faith. That faith, as the Apostle Peter was able to witness out of his own experience, is "more precious than gold which though perishable is tested by fire" (I Peter 1:7).

So it was God's love which stood behind this test of faith. Because of His fatherly concern, He wanted to lead us in this particular way. For God wants our faith to become "precious" through testing. Then our joy and our crown in heaven will be greater. God always has in view our destiny throughout all eternity. He knows that the more our faith is tested and proved here, the more we will be permitted to see up there. Faith here corresponds directly to sight up there.

37. The Untouchable Savings Account

"How are the finances?" This is the first question a Sister asks if she has been away for a few days, or comes home late in the evening after the day's gifts have been announced. Because, of course, the finances affect the continuance of all branches of our work. Each day following the noon meal our Sisterhood marches around the inner court of the Mother House. One of the Sisters carries a banner which has one of God's promises written on it. And then we also bring to the Father in heaven our most acute needs, together with this song:

> All our money comes from Him
> Who heaven and earth hath made,
> And even though we're sinners,
> No debt shall be unpaid!

We also sang this way after the Jesus Joy Retreat House was finished. The monthly payments were high, and it seemed there would be no end of them. For a long time I had hung up in my room all the bills that were outstanding, so I would see them continually. For these must be constantly presented in faith to the Heavenly Father. Evening by evening, up to the end of the month, I crossed out what could be paid, and wrote behind each sum a "thank you" to the Father.

But no sooner is one month past, than the bills for the next month rise up without mercy. From this viewpoint one can somewhat grasp the rumor that circulates about the Mary Sisterhood, that they enjoy nothing so much as a gift of money!

At a time when we were very short on money, God suddenly laid it heavily upon my heart to build the Jesus Proclamation Chapel. There was an urgency about it, too. He was waiting for us to become heralds for Him, broadcasting His message. This chapel, with its 1200 seats, would be dedicated to this purpose. In a little way I felt like King David who prayed, "I will not enter my house or get into my bed . . . until I find a place for the Lord, a dwelling place for the Mighty One of Jacob" (Psalm 132:3,4). But as long as we still owed payments on the Jesus Joy Retreat House, it was impossible to start a big project like this. It would cost nearly a quarter of a million dollars.

This command of God, however, was like a fire which cannot be extinguished by reason and sober calculations. It pressured me to take the next step in faith. One evening I said, "We are going to open a new savings account — for the Jesus Proclamation Chapel. Whatever is paid into it cannot be touched. It will be the down payment for the chapel, which we will begin in a very short time."

The Sisters raised some questions. Surely, many would give for this chapel — but what would be taken from what would otherwise go to our general fund, or the payments on our guest house, and —

However, I was certain that God Himself was the driving force behind the Jesus Proclamation Chapel. If He wanted it built in a hurry, then He would see that our other payments could be made on time, in spite of this new savings account. This touched the hearts of all the Sisters, and on my birthday they presented me with the new savings book.

Several days before, during the general devotion, I had presented this matter to the Heavenly Father in "faith verses." If this was to be a birthday present, then the savings book should not be empty or half empty — it should be full! I didn't know, however, that a savings book has space for seventy-eight entries. So if the Father wanted to fulfill this wish, seventy-eight gifts would have to come in a single day!

When the birthday celebration was over, and all the gifts had been entered, the last space was filled. More than thirteen hundred dollars had come in, though none of our friends knew about our little agreement with heaven. The cornerstone for the Lord's House was there! God had pledged Himself to it. In the following months this account continued to grow, and yet

95

we were able to meet all of our regular obligations.

Naturally there were some tight corners. And for the Sister in charge of the treasury, this was a special test. It was the first time she was exposed to the temptation to "borrow" from another account. In other situations this is often possible, but it could not be permitted here because this account had been sanctified to the Lord in a special way, and could not be touched. The time came to go ahead with our plans. We secured a building permit and discussed a financing plan with the contractor. The down payment required was precisely the amount which had accumulated in our "untouchable savings account."

Since that time we sing with even greater conviction, "He makes us bold in faith" — to believe something for His Kingdom. We saw how God waits for such faith and prayer. He answered the prayer for the full savings book, right up to the seventy-eighth entry. He let us build up the savings account without having to touch it for other expenses. He provided the down payment when it was time to begin construction. Truly, we have a great God. He loves to give great gifts. And therefore He rejoices when we are able to sense precisely where He wants to give us something. If we then honor Him with our faith and prayer — dwelling upon His power and His love — He will manifest His greatness.

GOD ANSWERS THE PRAYER OF BROKEN AND CONTRITE HEARTS

38. "King Balthazar" in the Year 1959

GOD LAID HIS FINGER on a very tender spot. He began to ask us about our love in the light of I Corinthians 13. He had to talk earnestly to us about this on a number of occasions, ever since we started our building work. Now, however, the

Father seemed to go after it with new force, as though He wanted to create something new.

Then it became clear to me that we should build a small nursing home at the same time we were building the Jesus Proclamation Chapel. In this Francis House we would care for old and needy people — putting into daily practice what we were proclaiming in the Jesus Proclamation Chapel. Nothing stands on a single leg. The counterweight to the proclamation of the word should be a practical expression of love — this is what the Lord had laid on my heart.

A long and fervent prayer battle ensued, concerning this love. With Christians, a house should always be built from the inside out! This means that a brick house, if it is properly built, will be placed like a "wrapping" over a spiritual construction which has been put there beforehand. So before we began to build the Francis House, there was this spiritual struggle over the issue of real compassion. We could not go on living if we did not have people with us whom we could help — that is the way I felt. When this desire reached a high point, then it would be certain that the Lord would erect a house overnight. That kind of thing He can do quickly, once the preconditions are fulfilled.

Most of the Sisters took this "overnight" as an hyperbole. But all of them knew that as long as nothing happened in regard to the nursing home, it meant that there had been no repentance, and therefore no real compassion among us.

Then came a time when we began to sense the judgment and wrath of God in many ways. Judgment blows and punishments broke over us. There was sickness and death. Our mission seemed to be going down like a sinking ship. Our garden, which supplies the major part of our noonday meal, was eaten up by insects and almost ruined. The promises of God seemed to be buried. The sum of all His dealings with us seemed to be the word in James 2:13, "For judgment is without mercy to one who has shown no mercy."

Now deep repentance broke out among us. We sensed that no sin weighs so heavily as the sin against love. We cried out to the Lord that He would give us love — He who is love, and who secured it for us on His cross as a precious gift. The goal of our faith was to obtain the kind of love spoken of in Sirach 40:24, "A brother helps a brother in need, but compassion does far more!" The Lord had given this to us as a Scripture for the entire year.

Then came Christmas, 1959. In my heart was a longing that the Lord would give us a "Bethlehem" on Christmas Eve. It should be a time when we come to Him as the shepherds and kings once came, to kneel at His manger and worship. Yes, adoration such as the shepherds and kings had brought — that we would bring now. Only one thing we could not bring — the gold which one of the kings had brought. It would have to be only incense and myrrh. The king, who would bring the gold, would have to be someone else. And I told my daughters that the Christ-child would surely rouse a king who would bring gold to His manger in order that the Francis House could be built. I felt that the Father in heaven, on this festival of His love, wanted to show that love as He had shown it that first Christmas. Nothing would have overjoyed us more than to receive an answer concerning the Francis House, for which we had prayed so continuously. And so I believed that the Lord had prepared this special joy for us.

We began to reckon firmly in faith that the prayer would be answered. Could we do this when our love was not perfect? We know that here on earth we never achieve perfect love, or a state of sinlessness. God expects one thing — a broken heart, which weeps over its sins. And God had broken us. But now Christmas had come, which speaks of God's mercy. Eternal love has come down to earth, in order that once again we might learn to love. Jesus is the surety for it, for He is the "wellspring of love." And so we dared ask the Lord for the Francis House on this Christmas festival. Indeed, we felt certain that "a king would appear" — that God in His mercy would let us experience a miracle gift this Christmas.

And what happened? When Christmas Eve came we knelt around the manger. We sang a song about kings and the gifts they brought the Christ-child. Then one of the Sisters waved an incense container. It gave forth no incense fumes, but within

98

was a precious envelope. What kind of a gift for the Christ-child did it contain? The day before one of the "kings" really had come, "King Balthazar" as we called him, and he had sent us a check for nearly ten thousand dollars for the building of the Francis House.

Words could not describe how overwhelmed we were that the Father in heaven had answered our Christmas prayer so exactly. It was almost too much to take in. During these Christmas days "King Balthazar" had actually knelt at the manger in our Assembly Hall, a living illustration of the word, "Before they call I will answer" (Isaiah 65:24). His "chamberlain," who was a friend of our Sisterhood, brought him to us. We had no acquaintance with him before that. This friend told him something about our work and the plans for the Francis House. During the celebration around the Christ-child, his heart was gripped with the conviction that the Francis House should be built at once. And so he wanted to make up whatever was lacking to erect a Swedish prefabricated house. The poor and the sick should have a pleasant home, and it should be done quickly!

This pretty little prefabricated house was built in two weeks. By the next fall it was standing there all ready, and a happy little "family" of old and sick people moved in. So God had let us experience a Christmas such as we had rarely experienced before — truly a festival of love. We, the failures and the sinners, had been permitted to have a real taste of His compassion. Without any merit on our part, He had heard our prayers and given us the Francis House. And with this gift He showed us that He has mercy upon repentant sinners who submit to His judgments, and that He accepts the prayer of a broken and a contrite heart.

39. The Filling Station Law

THE JESUS PROCLAMATION CHAPEL had been the object of our prayers for a long time. The model and all the plans had now been successfully completed by the architect. Some of the building materials already lay at the site. The building crane was ready to be delivered. And yet we could not begin work on it.

Right next to our property was a fair-sized field. It belonged to a businessman, and bordered directly on the highway. At that time he did not want either to sell or trade. He was negotiating with a big oil company which wanted to lease the land. They planned to erect a large filling station, with garages, restaurant, car wash, and so on. Quite understandably the building authority had not issued a building permit. They were not anxious to see a filling station and a church erected within 600 feet of each other. As long as the situation was not cleared up we were not able to begin construction. The other man was in no hurry, but we had no more time to lose.

The owner of the property started a suit against the city, in order to get a permit to build the gas station. The city authorities saw at once that the suit was almost certain to win. Their objections were not sufficiently valid. Close friends who had experience in such legal matters told us that the situation was impossible. There was no hope of a solution in favor of the Jesus Proclamation Chapel.

In our despair we called to the Lord day and night. The contractor was ready to haul his machines away and start on another building. He could return in perhaps half a year, if we had everything settled. We knew that our lack of repentance must be the reason that God had once more placed His chapel in jeopardy. A large gas station right in the middle of our "Canaan" for all time to come — that would be a monument to our sins. By no amount of imagining could we even dream of a solution. And God was silent.

In the meantime, the owner's suit came up on the court calendar. Now the State of Hesse, in which we live, had passed a law which said, "in residential districts no more filling stations shall be erected." We learned afterward that this law had actually been prepared for years, but had not been officially enacted. Just "by chance" it had become valid the day before the trial. The result was that the suit was dismissed, and nothing further stood in the way of building the Jesus Proclamation Chapel.

Three years later we were able to buy this neighboring piece of property from the owner. And the miracle was, there were no broken relationships, no resentments. But God had taught us something new through His intervention: in order to go the way of the Sermon on the Mount, we must renounce legal rights and the use of power; we must never initiate a lawsuit. And indeed, it was clear to everyone who observed this particular situation, that we never could have obtained the property by any leverage of power or legal processes. We obtained it solely because our Helper, Attorney, Manager, Father, and Advisor is the Almighty God Himself.

GOD ANSWERS PRAYER IN A VENTURE OF FAITH

40. The Occupation of "The Land Of Canaan" Near Eberstadt

To THE SOUTH of our Mother House stretched a broad land. Up to the year 1955 it lay largely undeveloped. Occasionally a wide strip of land would be planted to grain, or narrower strips to clover and sugar beets. But most of the land was green unplanted fields.

This lovely, countrylike area is bordered on the east by a federal highway and on the west by a large forest. It extends to the outlying houses of the suburb of Eberstadt. A little further on rise the wooded hills of the Oden Forest. Atop one of the hills can be seen the ruins of the Frankenstein Castle — the robber king of the Oden Forest.

The many birds and animals of the woods and fields around us made it hard to imagine that the city was so near. It was a place for quiet walks. The bells of both the Catholic and Lutheran church towers in Eberstadt would ring out over the land every evening. Certainly no one thought that this pastoral scene would soon be changed. But a big housing project and a freeway were being planned.

Through the years we had enjoyed the beauty of this setting. We lived in the city and yet in the country — between traffic and solitude, highway and forest. Up until now none of us had taken any interest in who owned the land, or in any plans which might be afoot for developing it. Our only instance of concern had been when a bypass road was under consideration, which would have affected our land.

A commission from God . . . for His glory

And then came the fourth of May, 1955 — the day on which the Lord gave me the inner conviction that He wanted to give us this land. There a "Land of Canaan" should rise up, a land of His promises and miracles. A foretaste of the kingdom of God, as a kingdom of love, should become visible and evident right here on earth. And so it was given me to work for the possession of this land, for God had laid His hand upon it for the purposes of His Kingdom.

All of the work which God had given us required room and buildings. We needed a large chapel to accommodate the crowds that came to see our Proclamation Plays. We needed a new guest house for the increasing numbers of people who came to our retreats. We needed facilities to help those who came to our door with physical needs. We needed space where we could do practical services of love for the old and infirm.

But, above all, did not the Lord on this day look forward

102

to a Land of Canaan among us which would proclaim His miracles, because land and buildings would be given alone through the help of God? Did He not look forward to a land which would speak in visible terms of the *reality* of God? Did He not desire to show His fatherly love — His abundant provision for His human children who live in complete dependence upon Him? Was it not the intention of His love to demonstrate that despite the fact that we were unprotected in every way, without insurance or steady income, nonetheless under His fatherly care we could live as in Paradise, in His peace and in great joy?

So now it became a question of taking possession of a promised land, a true "Canaan." The way into this promised land would be the way of prayer and faith. We believed that God would give us the victory, and we began by expressing this in a joyful act of faith. One of the first evenings after I had told my daughters about this great commission of God, we marched around our "promised land" like the children of Israel around Jericho. We carried little flags of faith, with the promises of God written on them, and we sang songs of faith and victory. A little boy who lived in the house at the far end of the land poked his head out the window and called, "Papa, come and see! The Mary Sisters are on maneuvers!"

And so the conquest of this land was proclaimed, and with it began a new campaign of faith of great dimensions. Just how great this campaign of faith would be, we did not at once realize. The land looked all of a piece, and the various meadows and fields just seemed to belong together — until one saw the land maps in the City Surveyor's Office. The land was divided into many tiny parcels. Many owners, with their relatives and heirs, often shared title to even a tiny strip of land. But at the time we knew nothing of this. I only knew that the Lord had given me confirmation for this new commission with the word —

Do not let them enter their cities; for the Lord your God has given them into your hand. (Joshua 10:19)*

*See footnote, page 12.

And this was further confirmed when God gave Mother Martyria the same inner conviction. We must hold fast this goal of faith, and allow ourselves no rest, until His promises be fulfilled, and a land rise up here for the sake of His Kingdom, a true Canaan in which He would be glorified.

And so we were given the watchword to enter into a battle of faith and prayer. Never before had we encountered such strong bulwarks. Never before did the battle go on so long, seeming never to end. The bulwarks seemed well-nigh invincible. In the years that followed they seemed to rise up almost without number. Every time one would fall, another would take its place, often more formidable than the one before. Up until now an effort of prayer and faith had brought help in a matter of days or weeks, or months at the most. But not so in the conquest of our land of Canaan. No, this was to be a long way, a way of faith which we must travel for years.

The Holy Scripture gave us clear direction for this. The journey of the children of Israel to Canaan stood before us — a long way through the wilderness in which God wanted to accomplish one thing: to prove their faith and to make them humble themselves (Deuteronomy 8:2). The goal of faith before us was tremendous: a land of God in which a "people of Israel" should be a living portrayal of a holy people, a light shining abroad into many lands. The goal could not be reached through any lesser struggle than theirs. And this journey of faith through the wilderness would also be God's time for training and disciplining us, as the Lord Himself describes this way: "As a man disciplines his son, the Lord your God disciplines you" (Deuteronomy 8:5). For the Land of Canaan is the land of God. God Himself desires to shine into and through the lives of its inhabitants. And so he makes it truly a "Holy Land."

God led His people Israel by these laws. They are valid for all ages. We could expect nothing else. In a small way, our wilderness journey would be a shadow of Israel's wilderness journey. In no other way could our Land of Canaan come to manifest something of His Kingdom, the kingdom of love.

And how did the wilderness journey of God's people to Canaan begin? With a miracle! They crossed the Red Sea dry

104

shod. The Lord also graciously allowed our way to begin with
a miracle. It came after a night of prayer, and launched us
on our wilderness journey. In the dark days which would follow, this first miracle again and again encouraged us to believe
that God would complete what He so wondrously began. When
we had traveled the hard road of faith through the wilderness,
He would let us see and possess the land of promise.

God's marvelous intervention as we start into the wilderness

This first miracle, which launched our journey of faith through
the wilderness, occurred on June 1, 1955 — three weeks after we
had received the inner commission for this battle of faith. It
took place in the conference room of Professor Peter Grund,
the Chief City Engineer. We had made an appointment with
him to speak about the land which we wanted. Right at the
outset of our conference he was called out of the room. We
sat down by the long conference table. Our eyes grew bigger
— and our hearts heavier — for spread out on the table was a
scale model of a sprawling development of high-rise apartments,
single dwellings, lawns, parking lots, and right down the middle
of it what looked like an express highway. We saw at once
that this model was for the land which we were calling our
"Canaan." We had come to get permission to develop this
land. And now we saw that the die had already been cast.

We could scarcely recover from our shock. When the Chief
Engineer returned, we laid our request before him, and then
heard from his own mouth the crushing fact which we already
knew, that the City Building Authority was ready to dispose
of this land — our Land of Canaan — according to the design
of the model. The Chief Engineer explained the plan to us.
Our neighbor, next to the Mother House, would be an American
Officers' Housing Project. The City Administration had already
pointed out to the Americans in a 16-page letter why they could
build only here and nowhere else. The City Engineer had drawn
up this plan himself, and therefore had a special interest in seeing it through. Beside the American settlement, the City Building Authority had parceled out our Land of Canaan for an ur-
gently needed middle-class housing project. As a matter of fact,

the ground-breaking ceremony for the American settlement was scheduled in just two weeks. All the arrangements for construction had been completed. Besides all these facts, a big bypass highway was planned right through the middle of this land. This was outside the authority of the City of Darmstadt. It came under the jurisdiction of the Federal Government in Bonn, and the plan was quite settled.

And so it seemed we must leave with nothing accomplished — and yet we couldn't, for God had given us a commission, a promise, and for these we had to battle in faith. In the Mother House a prayer battle was fought during this hour. These prayers loosed my tongue and gave me eloquence to lay our plans before the City Engineer once again: God desired to have this Land of Canaan, He had already laid His hand upon it, therefore it must be ours at all costs. Despite all the obstacles which had been raised, I walked around the entire model and emphasized that we must have this land without any restrictions because of the many and varied commissions which we had from God.

And what happened? As I spoke, the City Engineer suddenly took a piece of paper and a black crayon, and sketched a layout for the first houses on our Land of Canaan. God proved His word that with Him nothing shall be impossible! He had touched the heart of this man! The City Engineer said that he would not venture to oppose a plan such as ours. True, it was revolutionary and well-nigh impossible. But he felt that prayers and faith are great powers.

A miracle had occurred. God had changed the mind of the most influential person in the Building Administration. Despite fixed plans, he had become convinced that God wanted a "Canaan" to rise up on this land. Indeed, God had now prepared this man to upset these fixed plans, and to intervene with the authorities on behalf of Canaan even against his own interests.

And then we experienced the unforgettable sixth of June. For weeks the City Engineer had been scarcely available for even a few minutes' phone conversation. But on this day he drove out to our place. We all came together in our yard. It was a gorgeous day. Circled about by all the Mary Sisters, Professor Grund took a parchment paper out of his breast-pocket. He unfolded a tracing which he had drawn up quickly since seeing us last — a more elaborate design for the layout of Canaan. A beautiful row of trees ran through the middle, leading to the chapel for our Proclamation Plays which had an impressive outdoor stage. All the houses which we had thought of for Canaan and had told him about stood there before our eyes. With just a few strokes he had given form to our faith. Indeed, so realistic was it, that many of the Sisters suddenly realized how full of doubts they had been! It was almost like a dream. We could scarcely take it in.

Yet despite our great joy, a fearsome spectre rose up before us. During our conversation, God had changed the heart of the City Engineer. But would the City Council give its consent? The City Engineer emphasized over and over that the City Council must agree with our request. And our request was unheard of — making available land which had already been designated for another purpose. From a human standpoint there seemed no hope. The decisions regarding the Land of Canaan were already fixed. And he himself could plan nothing for this piece of land without the consent of the City Council.

The way through the wilderness had begun.

Great obstacles because of the greatness of God's plans

The way now called for visits to the city councilmen. Mother Martyria and I began a series of visits to each councilman, so that we could inform each one separately prior to the next Council meeting. The Lord gave us two words of Scripture:

Those blessed by the Lord shall possess the land (Psalm 37:22).

Fear not, and be not dismayed at this great multitude; for the battle is not yours but God's (2 Chronicles 20:15).

The visits with these men, however, did not go well. Most of them had no appreciation for our plan, which was certainly understandable from their viewpoint. Indeed, they were somewhat displeased that we even dared present such a request. So these visits were a great humiliation for us.

This was but the first four weeks of a faith battle which would last seven to eight years. The mighty hand of God was upon us, acting through men, to teach us patience and humility. It was a necessary discipline in our journey to Canaan. For when it was all over, we should not presume that by our own arm or our own faith we had done it. No, humbled and broken, we would then give the glory to God alone.

How many "children of Anak" (Numbers 13:33, Deuteronomy 9:2) had to lend a hand in breaking us, in order for us to learn faith under God's tests! The City Administration had established a municipal option over this piece of land. No party could purchase or develop any part of it unless the city would forego its option. Then there was the State of Hesse to deal with. It owned two-thirds of the land and had its own plans for the housing projects. Besides, about twenty private owners held small parcels of the land, and not all of them held sole title. In some cases a whole network of heirs held joint title to a tiny parcel of land, and usually it took a generation or more before they could all get together and agree on selling. The total area amounted to about 24 acres. The last and greatest obstacle, as already mentioned, was the plan of the Federal Government in Bonn to build a large, noisy highway right through the middle of our "promised land."

People who knew about the situation laughed at us and our "childish venture." "The Mary Sisters—" smiled a responsible official in Darmstadt; "They think that by faith even federal highways can be moved!"

More and more we experienced how daring and great this goal of faith was—to acquire the land around us as a "land of Canaan." We sensed that this would require a bold faith, a tenacious and patient faith, a faith that would not become weary in the face of all the opposition. Yes, it was a school of faith in which the learning was terribly hard. Yet we were strengthened by the certainty that the harder the path of faith, the greater the miracles that God performs. Thereby the honor of His name would be made great, and He would be glorified. And this was the very purpose for which we were to acquire the Land of Canaan.

The journey of the people of Israel through all temptations was a constant comfort to us. For this example in Holy Scripture showed us that the path we were traveling was the right one. The history of the people of Israel told us that great things would happen on such journeys of faith through the wilderness.

We would be cleansed and prepared, so that we could live in His land according to His Spirit. And then the kingdom of love would shed abroad its light. This gave us courage not to become weary in faith. The way often became dark. One *No* followed another. Sometimes it seemed that God Himself fought against us as we journeyed this pathway. But all the while He bore in His heart this plan for our discipline and growth.

His Word — an irrevocable promise

Then came an unforgettable day. A letter from the City Administration! My heart trembled as I opened it. It contained the verdict of the City Council meeting — the end result of all our pleas before the Mayor, City Manager, and councilmen. As I read the letter, the bottom seemed to fall out and my heart became heavy. According to the enclosed plan, the city had given us option on less than half the land — assuming that the private owners and the State of Hesse would sell it to us in the first place. But this was not all: the bypass highway formed the border of this land optioned to us. They had as good as denied our request. With this decision it was all over. It would be altogether impossible to have our chapel and prayer houses right next to a bypass highway, with all its traffic noise. Yes, it seemed to bring Canaan and its mission to naught.

In my prayer corner, I laid out this fateful letter with tears before God, my Father. I pled with Him to help us in our need. Had He not always stood behind His promises? And even the more so when His Kingdom was involved, as it was with us? In answer to this prayer I received this word of Scripture: "What man of you, if his son asks him for bread, will give him a stone? Or if He asks for a fish, will give him a serpent?" (Matthew 7:9,10). Encouraged by this promise of God, I took a pencil and crossed out the border and the bypass highway on the plan which had been sent to us.

I went to the Sisters in our Fellowship Hall and told them that the city had not granted our request. At the same time I showed them the plans on which I had crossed out the border and the bypass highway. I announced to them that the Father in heaven would move the border, according to the word of Scripture which He had given me at prayer. The whole of

Canaan would be ours. The word and the will of God cannot fail of fulfillment. He had given the word, "What man of you, if his son asks him for bread, will give him a stone . . . ." In order to carry out the commissions He had given us, we had prayed for a place of quiet. A noisy bypass highway would surely be "stones"! The Father in heaven would not give us stones! For where, where, where would you find an earthly father who would give stones? Where? Nowhere! How much less the Heavenly Father!

From that time on we sang to our Heavenly Father, again and again —

> Where is a father who gives stones instead of bread?
> Where, where, Where?
> Nowhere!

His word is Yea and Amen. That was my comfort in these days. Truly, the word of God has greater authority and is more certain than any word or decision of the highest human authorities. This alone gave me courage to continue along this dark pathway of faith through the wilderness. It could not but lead to a new revelation of God. For on dark pathways of faith through the wilderness, His word always speaks of *an end* — " . . . to do you good in the end" (Deuteronomy 8:16).

A particular song had come to us when we first received the commission to occupy Canaan. We continued to sing it bravely:

> The bypass highway cannot stand,
> The bypass highway cannot stand,
> The Lord has marked it for Canaan land!

From here and there we kept hearing that the date had been set to begin construction on the bypass highway. For a long time our prayers and songs of faith received no answer. Yet we continued.

Then one day the Lord reminded me of a former college teacher of mine. I had run into him the year before.

"If ever I can be of service to you," he had said, "or if I can help in any requests of the Mary Sisterhood, please let me know." So I called him up. In the meantime he had become Minister of Education for one of the states of the Federal

Republic of Germany, and he set himself to use his influence to help us

For a long time we heard nothing. Various petitions to high authorities in Bonn proved fruitless. They all shook their heads and said, "Impossible!"

But one day in February, 1956, a Sister was waiting in the Public Works Department. Her eyes fell on a layout plan which she scarcely dared believe: the bypass highway was redrawn far back into the forest!

Our chapel bells began to ring and seemed as if they couldn't stop. We ran around like ants in an anthill, greeting each other, dizzy with joy—

"The bypass highway's been moved! The bypass highway's been moved!"

God had made His promise come true: "Where is a father who gives stones instead of bread? Where, where, where? Nowhere!" Our joy and thanks to the Father knew no bounds on this great day of answered prayer.

Temptations put faith to the test

We had received a bolstering of our faith. Like the children of Israel, we had received "manna in the wilderness." But as we traveled further, neither were we spared the suffering. That was also part of Israel's wilderness journey. The way through the wilderness— then and now— is always a way fraught with temptations. In the wilderness one meets the Tempter. He latches on to our natural desire to have things easy and comfortable. He asked us, "Couldn't you have gone another and easier way? Perhaps this is a self-chosen way! Could you not better have remained where you were?" Such were the temptations he threw up before us. It was the old story: "You should have stayed with the flesh pots of Egypt!"

The Enemy had well prepared temptations along our pathway. One of our opponents had a friend on the City Council. This man now influenced the members of the Council with arguments which appeared quite "spiritual"— they would actually do us a good turn by refusing our requests. The smaller our work remained, the greater blessing it would be. If the work became large, it would become ineffective and unfruitful. One could see such a pattern in many similar works. Nor was this argument without its effect. Voices of opposition began to mount. Even our friends began to question whether our way were not a "tempting of God."

They had no way of knowing what a temptation was kindled by this new argument. Nothing would have pleased our old natures more. How lovely to stay small! Our battle for Canaan would be over. The gifts of our friends would more than meet current expenses for our present commitments. Wasn't the goal set simply too high? Should we really see this struggle through?

But God had spoken differently to us than these voices that rose up around us. He had given our Sisterhood this word of Scripture for the year 1957: "Behold, I have set the land before you; go in and take possession of it" (Deuteronomy 1:8). This word glowed as a bright star of promise in the dark night of temptation. It was a promissory note from God. Again and again we must present it to Him in faith and prayer.

At the beginning of the year, however, it seemed this word had little chance of fulfillment. In February, 1957, the whole matter of Canaan appeared darker than ever before. Indeed, our word of Scripture seemed like a taunt of the Enemy. Three days in a row discouraging news reached us — each report graver than the one before. It seemed that every spiritual nerve lay raw and exposed. We were told that the city was going to exercise its option on Canaan. We would not be permitted to buy anything there. Not even the privately owned fields could be sold to us. Furthermore, the purchasing contracts with private owners, negotiated at great pains, had to be canceled. Under no circumstances could we gain possession of further pieces of the land — either by trade, lease, or purchase. The hand of God lay heavy upon us in other ways also. Even the most joyful and lighthearted Sisters seemed half paralyzed by grief.

Was it not indeed so, that through the *No* of the authorities, God had in fact spoken His own *No*? Would so many people come after all — to visit Canaan or to live on it? These were dark days and weeks for us, as voices of discouragement continued to assault us.

In these weeks of great tribulation and temptation, I pleaded

112

with the Lord: *Show us Thy way! This is our only desire — to go Thy way!*

Did He truly want us to expand? In these days He gave an overwhelming answer through two Scriptures:

> And I will multiply upon you man and beast; and they shall increase and be fruitful (Ezekiel 36:11).
>
> For I am watching over my word to perform it (Jeremiah 1:12).

So we continued our wilderness journey. It had lasted almost two years now. Only prayer and faith kept us going in the hard and seemingly futile struggles. Indeed, the more impossible the conquest of Canaan became, the more the entire Sisterhood was driven to prayer. Groups of Sisters, and sometimes the whole Sisterhood, would wrestle in prayer all day long, and many times into the night. Always there was new repentance and cleansing, as God continued to discipline our Sisterhood.

Tenth birthday: "My Father, how good Thou art!"

The tenth birthday of the Mary Sisterhood drew near — March 30, 1957. For ten years we had experienced the overflowing goodness and love of God. This would have to be a day when His name as *Father* would be exalted as never before. Yes, we had tears. The night of faith seemed dark around us. Yet faith said — *nevertheless!* Nevertheless, a "Thanksgiving Festival to the Father like none before!" So it seemed right to us.

What would the Father in heaven do on this "His day"? Oh, some of us may have thought we knew something of His fatherly heart. But on this day we had to confess that we had not begun to truly comprehend His fathomless love. This is what happened.

The Festival worship service was over. At noon we gathered together with our several hundred guests and sang songs of praise. The songs had been written for the occasion. They recounted the fatherly love and goodness of God over the past ten years. The sound of praise and thanksgiving rose up as though it didn't want to stop. At four o'clock the Festival congregation gathered again in the Mother House Chapel. The Sisters had prepared a little play. It portrayed the miracles we had experienced during the building of our Mother House and Chapel — to speak and sing into our hearts the Father's great mercy.

But the Festival Play could not begin, for I was suddenly called out. Professor Peter Grund, the City Engineer who had stood so faithfully by us all these years, had arrived. His eyes twinkled with joy. He had brought a special gift for this Festival Day — a miracle gift from the Father. The City Council never met on Saturdays. Yet on this day — a Saturday, the tenth birthday of the Mary Sisterhood — they had held a conference. Our request concerning Canaan was discussed. And a miracle had occurred! Although the opponents had always been victorious before, they were suddenly outvoted. The decision was made that we should have first option on "the Land of Canaan." This meant that we could build on the land, if the State of Hesse and the private landowners would agree to sell. The City of Darmstadt had surrendered its option to us!

My heart sang out for joy, "My Father, how good Thou art!" I returned at once to the chapel, swinging a victory banner. Our whole program for the Festival was discarded. The goodness of God overwhelmed me. The joyful message had to be shared! A birthday present from the Father in heaven, which He had planned with fatherly love for this day and hour! I started the praise in free verses, which sang of this marvelous intervention of God in a hopeless siatuation. Immediately the entire congregation joined in on the refrain, praising the Father. And then we sang the blessing of God upon the City Engineer, Professor Grund, and also upon Mr. Daechert, the District Supervisor of Eberstadt, who had also supported us with the city authorities. We closed with the singing of "Great God, we praise Thee."

A word from the Lord shone brightly on this day. He had given it to us for our life in the Mother House, just before we moved in: "From of old no one has heard or perceived by the ear, no eye has seen a God besides thee, who works for those who wait for him" (Isaiah 64:4). Our diary for this day records that we were beside ourselves with pure joy — overwhelmed that the Father in heaven had thought to prepare this great joy exactly for the tenth birthday of the Mary Sisterhood. The songs of adoration to the Father's love, therefore, came out of overflowing hearts, and moved all of us deeply.

With the rerouting of the bypass highway, the first barrier to the occupation of Canaan had crumbled. Now a second wall came tumbling down. Thereby God had given us down payment on His promise in the Scripture of 1957: "Behold, I have set the land before you . . . ." And "down payment" meant that the full payment would come in its time.

Israel's journey through the wilderness lasted 40 years. How long would it be with us? With these two years it would not yet be finished. Our faith had not yet been sufficiently tested. We were not sufficiently humbled and prepared. It was not fitting that the great goal of a Land of Canaan should be reached by such a short journey of faith.

New humiliations and disciplines

The *No* of the city authorities had been changed to a *Yes!* They had given us first option to buy the land. But this was a far cry from actually having Canaan in our hands. We had bought a few narrow strips of land from private owners. But how small they were beside the large sections which still seemed impossible to obtain! The next obstacle was: the State of Hesse, which owned the largest share of the land. A new journey of faith through the wilderness began.

We literally paralleled the experience of the children of Israel. Their actual journey to Canaan could have been accomplished in a matter of weeks. Yet they had to wait at the doorway of the Promised Land, as it were, all those years. They wandered back and forth, sometimes virtually having a foot within the land, only to be beaten back again.

We had a decisive conversation with a high official in the state government. He told us that their plans were fixed. They would never sell us any part of Canaan. Altogether downhearted, Mother Martyria and I started toward home. What good was the birthday present we had received on our tenth anniversary? Fine that the City of Darmstadt had released its option to us — but what good is an option when nobody would sell us the land?

And now from another source we heard that the bypass highway was going to be routed through our land after all. Once again the situation seemed altogether hopeless.

1957-1959! No one could express in words what these years meant for us: the deepest temptations we had yet experienced . . . distresses . . . struggling through to ever renewed faith. We went all the way to the governor of Hesse with our petition. But at the end of it all, we held in our hand a final, written, decisive *No* from the state government. They would never sell us the land. And therewith the doom of all our hopes and plans seemed to be sealed.

In such times the Lord sends another kind of miracle. This kind of miracle is not so easy to relate as the kind where great obstacles to the occupation of Canaan were overcome. For these are the hidden, yet the true and essential miracles, which are wrought in our hearts. They come through discipline and waitings and humiliations. Above all, they come as we learn to humble ourselves deeper and deeper under our sins — our sins which cause the Lord such endless concern and effort.

As far as God were concerned, He could grant our requests quickly. But He must often prolong matters so that we do not occupy the Land before we are prepared. For the Land is holy, set apart for His purposes. If we were to storm in with our sinful ways, we would spoil it.

Waiting, waiting, waiting:
How will the wilderness journey end? Will faith persevere?

In this time we bowed low under the discipline and chastening of God. Yet we continued to present Him with His promises, with the sincere plea that He would not allow His glory to be brought to shame before the people. For thousands of people, both in Germany and abroad, receive our "Friendship Letters." As early as 1955 we had written that God had promised to give us this land of Canaan — a true Canaan, a land of His promises, a kingdom of love. Many eyes were focused on Canaan. Would God stand behind His promises? Should such faith projects be pursued? Does God approve of such audacious faith? Do such ways of faith truly magnify His glory and build

His Kingdom? So our struggle could not be a private one. It was like a public drama, acted out before heaven and earth.

What if God would not make good His promises? What if He would not speak His Yea and Amen to such ways of faith? Then something of faith in the promises of God would collapse for countless people. They would no longer have the courage to go such ways of faith in their own lives.

At this time all hope seemed to be extinguished. But then it was that the Lord kindled a new hope. He touched the heart of Mr. Daechert, the District Supervisor of the suburb of Eberstadt. Mr. Daechert had taken our part on previous occasions, and he had connections with high officials in the state government. In the midst of this deep distress, his heart became newly inflamed for God's cause. Our petition became his petition. From that time on he spoke of "our struggle." He committed himself to the utmost to bring Canaan into our possession.

Besides this, the Lord awakened the interest of one of the pastors who had conducted worship services for us over a number of years — Pastor Rathgeber. He was the supervisor of certain welfare and educational work in the Evangelical Church of Hesse. One day he suddenly took a personal interest in the difficulties we were having. He, too, committed himself in a selfless way to Canaan. He spoke to our Church president, Dr. Martin Niemoeller, who in turn spoke personally to the governor of Hesse about our Canaan project.

In spite of these rays of hope, months went by and the obstacles did not fall. But the Lord was showing us by this that we should continue on the pathway of faith. And in time the goal would be reached, for:

> What God has undertaken and what He desires, must inevitably
> arrive at His purpose and goal.

Again and again we struggled to stand on God's promises. For He had given such rich promises along this pathway of faith. Despite all the disappointments, we endeavored to hold these before Him in faith.

The "latter end" of God's mercy

But now God's hour drew near. The high government official, whose ironclad *No* stood as a main obstacle to our moving into Canaan, was moved to another position.

March, 1959. Another birthday of the Mary Sisterhood was at hand, our twelfth. The last official working day before Easter fell on March 29th. The telephone rang. The government official asked for the Sister who handled the property negotiations. The Sister who was our receptionist related afterward: "My heart leaped with excitement as I stood next to her. Sister Anita beckoned, covered the mouthpiece for a moment, and exclaimed, 'Ring the bells! The governor has signed the permit to complete the purchasing contract!'"

With this action all Canaan was ours. What a birthday present from the Father in heaven — and again on the anniversary of the Mary Sisterhood!

The decision had come at the last possible hour before the March 30th holiday. The long prayed-for, suffered-for and fought-for state property on Canaan had come into our possession. God had fulfilled His word. In the darkest hours, this had been my anchor of faith: God leads through the wilderness, "that he might humble you, and test you, to do you good in the end" (Deuteronomy 8:16).

Our knees could scarcely support us for trembling, when we heard the news. It was the greatest surprise — the greatest of His miracles — which our house had experienced since March 30, 1957. It took a little while before we could collect our senses and break out with "Now thank we all our God." What God had done! To this day, all those who followed even a little way on this journey to Canaan, can scarcely grasp it.

Other miracles followed on the heels of this miracle of the state property. Nearly all the private landowners, who at first could not be budged to sell, now consented to do so. Whereas before our requests had gone unheeded for months and years, now God had intervened. A large number of the private landowners came to us of their own accord and offered their parcels of land, so that today all of Canaan is truly ours.

"Canaan" — the land where God will be glorified

What do we see now in 1966, after eleven years of "Canaan

history"? Canaan is truly the land where the miracles of God have become visible. When we walk from our Mother House through the forest in the opposite direction from Canaan, we come to the housing development for American officers, lying directly on the highway. According to the "model," it was to have been built right in the middle of our land. But now, in its place, stands the Jesus Proclamation Chapel, which seats from 1000-1300 people, and was dedicated on May 14, 1961.

What a Lord! In the darkest hour He had given a word: "many people and beasts would be on this land." And how He fulfilled this word of promise!

More than 2000 people streamed to the dedication services. They spilled over the newly laid-out footpaths on Canaan in a great festival procession. Sisters with victory banners and instruments led the way, and the whole congregation joined in songs of praise and thanks.

Every second or third Sunday during the summer one of our Proclamation Plays is presented. Often more than a thousand people attend them and receive the message from *The Time Is Near:* The end times are upon us; prepare yourself! And so they are drawn into the celebration and spirit of life in Canaan, where God manifests His glory.

Other houses have been built in Canaan. The Francis House went up at the same time as the Jesus Proclamation Chapel, a house of mercy for the aged and infirm. Next to it a second small house, "Beth Zion," a hostel for our Jewish friends, is planned. At the far end of Canaan is the house called "Jesus' Comfort." Our Sisters of the Crown of Thorns live there, together with some old and infirm people, and some Friends of Canaan.*

Opposite the Jesus Proclamation Chapel, on the edge of the

---

*The Thorn Sisters belong to the Mary Sisterhood. They are women who cannot live together with us because of age, marriage, or job responsibilities. They live out the spirit of our commission wherever they are. The Sisters of the Crown of Thorns are a group of older women who have come to live with us and to share our life on Canaan. Friends of Canaan share a somewhat looser relationship with us. They share the spirit and burden of our calling. They hold chapter meetings of The Friends of Canaan in a number of cities.

forest, is the large Canaan Retreat House, Jesus' Joy, with fifty single guest rooms.

In all of these houses one can truly follow the admonition, "Sing to the Lord a new song, for He performs miracles!" For all who come here and live here find themselves in a land of fulfilled promises, this land of many miracles of God. They are gripped by the reality of our God and Father, who works miracles yet today.

And when one looks out over the broad land, something yet further grips him with astonishment. Here are more than twenty acres of high-priced urban land which had to be paid for, often simultaneously with the buildings which were being built upon it. Land and buildings ran to more than half a million dollars. These were some of the darkest hours of our Sisterhood. Our treasury operated day to day close to empty. How did it all happen? Only by the miracle ways of God.

The miracle Land of Canaan! God allowed us to acquire it, but only at great price, along dark pathways of faith, and through many testings. Nor do we any longer wonder why. For we see now that this is God's "Kingdom Land," Canaan! As the land had drunk in our tears during hard battles of faith, along difficult pathways of patience, and through many disciplines and punishments — so now it became to the same degree a land of joy and song, a land of adoration and festal dancing. Yes, now it is truly a land where the Father is praised. For at the end of the way He blesses abundantly. He allows the way of faith to end in a visible manifestation of His goodness. He makes a way through the wilderness into the Promised Land. He crowns the way of testing and tribulation with matchless fruit.

The way of faith through the wilderness to Canaan proves one thing: the more prayer and faith and suffering required, the more the Father gives. Yes, at the end of the way of faith, we are given to see His miracle power, His glory, His goodness. And the more we witness of these, the greater the effect for His Kingdom.

Canaan — kingdom of love! May it be that ever more and more in these difficult end times, to the glory of the Father, the Son, and the Holy Ghost.

ALL THESE REPORTS proclaim a single truth: "Prayer is power." People of prayer are invincible. They are not to be conquered by any enemy attack, by any resistance, by any suffering or difficulty in life because in their hands they carry the surest weapon for victory. Yes, with prayer they have been given the key to the Father's heart.

We hope these reports may give illustrative material for a little school in petitionary prayer. They show through practical life experiences how God bestows the gift of prayer upon His human children. Out of his great love He helps them so that in need or despair they are not thrown to the mercy of adversities, but can always receive help because prayer can change any situation, can change human hearts, can change *all things.*

Now the important question is, how to use this gift and weapon. Otherwise we remain at the mercy of our distresses. These stories show that the most diverse troubles and difficulties remain unchanged, when this weapon of prayer is not used. Jesus said, "*Ask,* and you will receive" (John 16:24). The promise of help is given to him who asks.

However, it is not enough that the weapon of prayer is simply used. It must be used *in the right way.* This is pointed up in several of the stories, where our habits of life proved to have a bearing on our prayers being answered or not being answered. Prayer *per se* does not bring help. Only the right prayer has His promise. This is a basic biblical truth, and we experienced it in a variety of needs and difficulties: When we did not pray properly no help and no answer came.

God binds Himself to His Word. He answers only such prayers as He has promised to answer because they are in harmony with His will. So it is very important that we learn how

121

we are to pray and in what situation the various kinds of prayer should be used.

No school, however, is as effective as the school of experience which is reported here.

What prayers are important to God? What prayers has He promised to answer? Or, expressed in a different way, which prayers have no promise of finding answers, and are therefore like a dull weapon which has no power and does not do anything? Which prayer has no authority?

Prayer Obstacles

In the school of prayer we must first clearly analyze the obstacles to prayer which are mentioned in the Holy Scripture. Scripture points out this decisive truth: when God does not answer, *our unrepented sin stands in the way and can form a barrier.*

> Behold, the Lord's hand is not shortened, that it cannot save,
>   or his ear dull, that it cannot hear;
> but your iniquities have made a separation
>   between you and your God,
> and your sins have hid his face from you
>   so that he does not hear. (Isaiah 59:1,2)

The New Testament names several sins which are prayer obstacles. This means that prayer has absolute prerequisites, and if these are not fulfilled the prayer is impeded. Above all, this includes the transgression of the Ten Commandments, according to Jesus' interpretation in the Sermon of the Mount. In general these are: refusal to forgive (Matthew 6:15); wrath and doubt (I Timothy 2:8); all sensuous, passionate behavior (I Peter 3:7, 4:7,8a); refusal to confess our sins one to another (James 5:16); stinginess and greediness, because, "give, and it will be given to you; good measure, pressed down, shaken together, running over" (Luke 6:38); earthly-mindedness, because "seek first his kingdom and his righteousness, and all these things shall be yours as well" (Matthew 6:33).

But now the questions arise: Who can pray and be heard? Who can say, "And we receive from him whatever we ask, because we keep his commandments and do what pleases him"

(I John 3:22)? Who can say that he is one of the righteous, of whom the Holy Scripture says, "The eyes of the Lord are upon the righteous, and his ears are open unto their cry" (Psalm 34:15 K.J.)? By these 'righteous,' God's Word does not mean people without sin, because they do not exist. On the contrary, it refers to sinners who repent of their sins and therefore partake of the atonement, and are renewed. Such will not go on in unforgiveness and bitterness, but will go and get reconciled. They will not remain in sin and lust, but will depart from such ways. They will not hold on to everything. They are the kind who are willing to let go and give — "and it will be given to them."

A decisive obstacle to answered prayer, therefore, is unrepented and unconfessed sin from which one does not want to depart. However, where sin is forgiven, and we can pray out of a humble and repentant heart, the Scripture's promise to the publican becomes our promise (Luke 18:13-14). In many of the stories told here this truth comes out. God's ears had apparently been closed to our prayers. Then suddenly, the petition was granted. What made the change? The Sisters who had been unkind or unforgiving in their attitude toward one another had changed. God does for us exactly what He has promised in His Word.

God, however, has not only bound Himself to His words concerning certain obstacles to prayer. He has also given special promises in regard to certain kinds of prayer. It is important, therefore, to learn the different kinds of prayer which God promises to answer. If we can learn to take hold of such prayer opportunities, we will have a position of power at His throne.

The Prayer of Faith

The first kind of prayer which God has promised to answer is "the prayer of faith." Jesus shows us that the granting of a petition indeed depends upon whether it is spoken in strong faith. The Word says, "It will be given to you according to your faith" (Matthew 9:29). God expects a daring faith, a mountain-moving faith. However, daring ventures of faith can only be undertaken in obedience to God. Abraham dared to step out on faith and emigrate to Canaan without knowing

123

whether he would find a home there, because God had so commanded him. He believed in God's guidance, and so he was obedient even in the face of uncertainties. Some of the stories told here testify to this same truth. A venture of faith was launched in obedience to God's command — and then God answered, and in answering He glorified Himself.

These reports show us from practical experience how the prayer of faith should be done. God does not expect that our faith should be vague or aimless. The faith must be in His Word. This is the strong anchor to which faith must be attached. The believer who has been given a promise from God had an IOU in his hand which he can present to God over and over again: "Father, Thou hast said, 'Give, and it shall be given to you.' Nobody shall perish who waits on Him!"

At times this promise may be a word from the Scripture, which God has quickened in a personal way at a time of difficulty or decision. With the prayer of faith it is especially important that we praise and thank and worship God, the Almighty One — indeed, that we sing out His praises even in a seemingly hopeless situation, for in thanksgiving we receive. Where we praise His almighty power, He lets His arm be moved; where His fatherly love is praised in song, His fatherly heart bends lovingly down to us.

Childlike Prayer

Childlike prayer has its special promise. Again and again Jesus admonishes us to become like children, for to them the Kingdom of heaven belongs, to them God's fatherly heart is open. They conquer the Father's heart by their childlike manner, as they come to Him with their smallest needs, asking for even the littlest things. Jesus says, "If an earthly father cannot give a stone to his child when he asks for bread — how much more will the Father in heaven do good to us, His children, when we come to Him in a childlike attitude of love and confidence." If such a prayer is according to His will, it will not be disappointed. It may be, of course, that He will hold back the answer to a prayer, if there is a specific obstacle hindering the prayer, such as we mentioned above. In doing this He will be teaching us, so that later He may give us even more abundantly.

The Scripture says, "You do not have, because you do not ask" (James 4:2). Is it not just this lack of childlike prayer that stands behind such a Scripture? We remain poor, with many needs, and cannot speak of answered prayer simply because we are too unchildlike to ask. Or, perhaps, we are so rich and well satisfied that we do not find ourselves in a situation where we must come to the Father and ask. God, however, wants to be a father to us. He wants us to come to Him with every one of our needs. He waits for children who will ask of Him time and time again, because as a loving father it is His joy to do us good and give us gifts. Many of the stories in this book testify to this. They seek to show that the heart of the Heavenly Father, which is pure love and care, is concerned about the smallest needs of His people, and that He answers their prayers.

Prevailing Prayer

The Scripture also encourages the worshiper, "be constant in prayer" (Romans 12:12). Our prayers should not be slack, for God's promise is also given to prevailing prayer. The persevering prayer does not become weary, will not let itself be repulsed, even when it sees no apparent fulfillment, but often the contrary. Persevering prayer has the ability to quietly persist, and to wait. This is a humbling kind of prayer. It humbles one to have to wait, and to have to ask again and again, "What is the reason that Thou canst not answer my prayer? Is there, perhaps, a sin barrier in my life?"

These stories, however, show that the outcome of persevering prayer is usually a truly miraculous answer from God. He manifests Himself in such a way that His greatness and power are magnified before men. Therefore, the persevering prayer also has His special promise. It allows great things to come to the petitioner who is purified by such byways of waiting, allows him to experience the mighty works of God.

With the persevering prayer God calls us to an effort, a struggle — such as we see in the case of the Phoenician woman or the insistent widow. It is a real wrestling with God, as with

Jacob at the Jabbok: "I will not let you go, unless you bless me" (Genesis 32:26). Such prayer pleases God. Jesus says that God will answer such prayer, "because of our importunity." Here, however, it must be emphasized that God gives assurances and answers in such a prayer-struggle only if these prayers are uttered in Jesus' name, and are of His mind and spirit. Self-willed prayers — for example, the prayer that a loved one be spared from death — have no promise of an answer.

For such a wrestling in prayer it is especially important that we take our stand on the promise and assurance which God has given, and then that we hold fast to the end. The stories tell about the acquiring of Canaan. The promise of God here was a rock foundation in a situation which was hopeless for many years. We have similar promises with petitions regarding the kingdom of God, and the salvation and sanctification of human souls. Such requests must always be in the name of Jesus. He will hear and answer them — but always in His own time. A zeal for God's kingdom, for God's glory, paves the way for the coming of His Kingdom and His victory. Therefore, such prayers are always according to His will and promise.

Earnest Prayer

The earnest prayer also has a great promise. The Scripture says that It accomplishes much (James 5:16). Indeed God has promised answer for this prayer in a special measure. As expressed in the word, earnest prayer is not glibly said, but it has received a special emphasis, a special underlining. It will be strengthened, made urgent, through small sacrifices and gifts of time, energy, goods and similar things. The stories show very impressively that in the most hopeless situations and needs which rose up to God day in and day out without an answer, these prayers were granted as they became earnest and were emphasized through various sacrifices and commitments. Therefore, how often our prayers cannot accomplish much with God because He cannot take them in earnest, for we are not in earnest about them! Otherwise, we would pray with a different emphasis and give our prayer more weight.

126

The Way to Prayer

In what way, however, shall we come to daring faith, to childlike trusting, to persevering and earnest prayer, and to prayer out of a repentant heart? Can only specially blessed people pray this way? No, God reveals these ways of prayer for all Christians. And in our Lord Jesus Christ they have all been manifested. It only means that we must make the next step in real life. I do not have to get worked up, but I must stand on the assurances which the Lord has given me by His Word, or personally in certain situations of need. Surely the gift of faith exists as a gift of grace from the Holy Spirit where great commitments in God's kingdom are involved. But Jesus says: "Therefore I tell you, whatever you ask in prayer, believe that you receive it, and you will" (Mark 11:24). And this pertains to every Christian for his prayer life.

And when we strive for the childlike prayer, this is not a difficult way either. All we have to do is to go with all our needs to the Father. We bring Him all of our distresses and requests in the confidence that He will grant them. And we will find that He knows what we need and answers our requests.

The key to prayer can also be learned and given to us if we take the next step — that is, if we underline it by some commitment which is shown to us by the Holy Spirit as a small sacrifice. Our Lord Jesus says: "But this kind never comes out except by prayer and fasting" (Matthew 17:21), and shows through it a way to earnest prayer with the help of fasting, which means to abstain from whatever represents to me a physical, spiritual or mental enjoyment.

Or with the prayer out of a purified heart it is important that I have confessed my sin and have not let any unforgiven sin stay between God and myself or other people. It means to take the next step and to cleanse myself wherever God puts His finger on my life, to ask God and men for forgiveness, and to depart from this or that — then the way to effective prayer is again free.

These testimonial reports about answered prayers paint God before our eyes as a father and show us how He waits only to be able to answer prayers. They tell us how great His love is toward us, His children, and how great His power is to make a change in situations of despair and impossibility. When Jesus admonishes us again and again to pray, it proves His loving promise that He will give us the grace of prayer. For Jesus does not demand anything from us which He does not give us at the same time. And has He not promised us the Holy Spirit to bring to us the grace of prayer? When we in our weakness attempt to pray, we should say, "I believe in the Holy Spirit!" We should call to Him. He will make pray-ers out of us.

In view of the love of the Triune God, who has given us the gift of prayer, may these reports encourage us to start with the various kinds of prayer or to get more practice in them. This way of prayer has been proven reliable by experience and leads to the goal. Everyone of us can therefore experience that we have a God who answers prayer, who performs miracles.